EMPOWERING
DREAMERS
To Become
Achievers

Living Your Life Without Fear
and Limitations

RAMSEY JAY, JR.

Words of Commendation for *Empowering Dreamers To Become Achievers*:

"In 'Empowering Dreamers To Become Achievers', Ramsey Jay, Jr. has given readers a potent, powerful and methodical way to transform their thinking and aspirations from uncertainties to accomplishments. This book will give any reader that push forward that we all need sometime."

— *Carla A. Harris, Vice Chairman, Global Wealth Management, Senior Client Advisor, Morgan Stanley, President Obama Appointee - Chair of the National Women's Business Council, Author of "Expect To Win" and "Strategize To* Win"

"Ramsey offers a uniquely insightful and deeply compelling approach to creating a successful life filled with meaning. Drawing upon his extraordinary personal journey and the wisdom gained through interactions with many mentors — including his grandmother — Ramsey urges us to boldly envision the life we want and take the necessary steps to make it a reality. I was inspired by his challenge to imagine seeing our most beloved mentor and to prepare to answer the question 'What did you do with the gifts I've given you?'"

— *Joseph I. Castro, Ph.D. M.P.P., President & Professor of Educational Leadership, California State University,* Fresno

"Life is full of opportunities. What you do with them often separates those who are successful from those that are not. Being prepared to make the most of your opportunities is what Ramsey's book is all about."

— *Les Biller, Co-founder of the Sheri & Les Biller Family Foundation, Retired Vice Chairman, Wells Fargo* Bank

DEDICATION

This book is the realization of one of my most purposeful dreams. Ever since I was a child, I have been enamored with enacting this well-intentioned rhetoric: "If you dream, you can do it." I am humbled and thankful that God has entrusted me with the gift of communication that allows me to be a blessing to others. Yet, I am also resolute that my abiding desire to make this book a reality is the result of the community of support that has shepherded me throughout my life's journey. Benjamin Disraeli once said, "the greatest good you can do for another is not just to share your riches, but to reveal to him his own."

I dedicate this book to three people—Mom, Dad and my beloved, promoted-to-heaven grandmother, Mary Lee Barrett—who not only shared their emotional, spiritual and intangible riches with me but optimistically championed and encouraged me to find the riches within myself. Your unconditional love, selflessness and faithful dedication to my dreams has propelled me to Keep Dreaming! You are my "Quintessential Motivators" and your familial fortitude and reverent dedication to my dreams allowed me to cultivate those very dreams. You showered me with love, emotional stability and words of unwaning encouragement, all while making the ultimate sacrifices in your own lives. You were my teachers, my guides, my sage advisors on matters that could not be taught in the classroom. You taught me humility, respect, dignity, honor, character, kindness and the importance of being "Obedient to the Call" on my life to serve others with the same grace and commitment you exemplified while nurturing me and helping to develop my character.

I lovingly salute and honor you Mom, Dad and my benevolent grandma for your inexhaustible efforts to embolden my dreams and help pave the path for me to leave an indelible footprint for those coming after me.

ISBN: 978-1-48356-406-7

TABLE OF CONTENTS

INTRODUCTION

I've never been comfortable accepting limitations, especially arbitrary ones. That's just not in my DNA. I'll give you an example. In 2000, I was a senior at California State University, Fresno. Fresno State is a perfectly good public university, but when I was a student there it was not one of the prestigious brand name schools that leading Wall Street firms recruited from, and I knew that I wanted to start my finance career with a Wall Street firm. Where did the leading banks and asset management firms recruit? Why, in northern California's Bay Area, of course. So that's where I went.

To be more specific, I heard about a financial job fair at Stanford University, one of the world's most prestigious institutions of higher learning. Of course, I didn't attend Stanford, but that was an arbitrary limitation to me. Was I less talented or deserving of an opportunity to compete for an interview because I attended a state school? I certainly didn't believe so. So up the state I drove.

I was one of the first *students* to arrive on campus and as I was walking into the job fair one of the recruiters stopped me. "Are you a student?" she asked.

I replied, "Yes." Technically, I was a student. Not a *Stanford* student, but a student majoring in finance nevertheless, with a dream to work at one of these premier financial institutions. Sensing the nature of my reply, she asked, "Are you a student enrolled here?" I replied, "Yes ma'am. I am a student who is enrolled, and I am here." Still unsatisfied, she eventually forced me to admit that I didn't attend Stanford.

Then she asked me a question I believe we must all purposefully answer in order to both protect and pursue our dreams: "Why are you here?" More specifically, why did I drive 200 miles across California? I told her it was my dream to work for one of these Wall Street firms, and this was where the companies were recruiting. In the words of Pat Hill, Fresno State's head football coach at that time, I told her I was just as qualified to compete against "anybody, anywhere, anytime." In this case "anybody" included my fellow students taking classes in those hallowed Palo Alto halls.

I wish I could confirm that the recruiter was so impressed by my moxie that I ended up landing my Wall Street dream job. However, that would not be true. I did get an interview, and my name and resume went into the candidate pool, but I didn't get hired. In retrospect, that was beside the point. The point was that I had defied limitations and done something bold in order to pursue my dream, and I was better for it. Taking that risk felt really, really good. Liberating, in fact. On that winter day in 2000, I realized I was pretty comfortable going out on a limb. I've made a habit of it ever since.

Learning from Phil and Sally Jessy

Ever since I was a little kid growing up in the vintage beach town of Ventura, California, I've been determined to become my own person—not to fit into a mold created by anyone else. As far back as I can remember, I didn't like cartoons but loved the daytime talk shows with hosts like Phil Donahue and Sally Jessy Raphael. I would sit in front of the television for hours, watching and replaying recordings of the shows, carefully listening to the hosts and their guests and mimicking their mannerisms. I studied how true professionals connected with a myriad of people in diverse environments, made them comfortable, and engaged in meaningful communication.

Even as a young boy, I gave myself permission to be the person I wanted to become: a communicator, someone who would throw out a lifeline for individuals—from adult professionals to youths from underserved communities—whose internal self-talk was all about what they could not have, could not do or could not be. Along the way, I discovered that if I developed both my mind and my eloquence, there was literally no limit to how far my desire and hard work could take me.

In the end, they took me all the way to Hanover, New Hampshire, home of Dartmouth College. There, in the small-town bosom of the Ivy League, I attended the Tuck School of Business and in 2005 graduated with my M.B.A. While I was at Tuck I had numerous life changing experiences, none more moving than being chosen by my classmates to deliver the commencement address at our graduation. I was humbled by the honor; this was a group of first-class leaders and business minds, men and women who have gone on to leave global footprints on Wall Street, Silicon Valley, government, health care and beyond. Yet they selected me to represent them, and I couldn't have been more honored.

Why did they choose me? I think, in part, it was because I had been honing my skills as a speaker practically since the day I arrived on the campus. Early on, I started telling everyone who would listen that I was passionate about refining my speaking and communication skills, and the more I spoke, the more my reputation and talents developed. With the simple act of stepping up and going beyond the traditional role of dutiful grad student, I became something of a leader to my peers. I also laid the groundwork for professional and personal relationships that thrive even to this day.

Who I Am

A decade later, those who know me would describe me as a renaissance man of sorts; someone who wears many hats. By day, I have helped manage investments for major institutional investors such as public and private pension funds, endowments, foundations, and family offices. It's challenging, fulfilling work that I am proud to do. I love being able to assist a multitude of people who work very hard, often in a service capacity, to enjoy brighter prospects for their financial futures. It's incredibly rewarding.

I am fortunate to have received excellent academic and practical training to become a first-rate financial executive. That said, my heart's passion resonates in my God-given gift as a S.W.I.T.E.P. (Speaker Writer Interviewer Teacher Emcee Producer). For more than a decade, I've built a career talking to groups ranging from elite business professionals to my favorite audiences: groups of young men and women, particularly those from underserved communities. All my audiences are important to me, but it's young people—many with a dream like mine—who compel me to do what I do. Corporate employees, civic leaders, nonprofit boards of directors, media and entertainment moguls all have used my advice on how to reclaim their dreams or bring about change in their lives, but the kids…the kids *need* me.

It is one thing to tell a younger person to have a dream, but it is something fundamentally different to empower them to realize that dream. Perhaps it's the unending blessings of my own childhood that have infused me with a spirit of hope and optimism for our youth. I am acutely aware that of some of our kids face unfavorable economic forces, a tattered social fabric, and a culture that seems to consider "making it" accessible only to people who come from certain zip codes.

Many of these young people, who are smart, talented and passionate, are also apathetic, disillusioned, and hopeless. But they're also filled with limitless potential, and I feel that I have a call on my life to remind them that in spite of everything, the power to change their lives and reclaim their dreams remains in the palms of their hands. I'm proud to say that when I finish addressing a room of students, there are usually more smiles and hugs than shoulder shrugs and eye rolls. I'm even prouder to say that with my encouragement, more than a few students have changed their lives. I'll share some of those stories in this book.

But why a book? Isn't print dead? Nobody reads anymore, right? Wrong. Books are still very much alive. In fact, as I started speaking before larger audiences, people would come up to me after I finished and ask me if I had a book. Over and over, I was asked, "Where's your book?" After a while, it became clear that my audiences were genuinely moved by what I was sharing with them and wanted to take a piece of it home. They wanted a tool to continue the learning process. In a sense, they craved a talisman of hope, a bit of proof that it was possible to build a better life and to bring one's dream to fruition.

This book is my gift to everyone whom I've touched in any way with my words. It's my way of saying thank you. Without you allowing my words to impact you, I wouldn't have ever known that what I was saying was so important to so many. Most importantly, it is because of you that I have been so committed to developing my message. I am profoundly grateful.

The X Factor

The book is also my exploration of a critical question that does not seem to have a clear answer in the mountain of self-development books that crowd bookstore shelves:

What makes people take action and make meaningful change?

That is probably the single biggest question in motivational speaking, self-help publishing, and even psychology. We know what to do to live more fully, make better choices and create the life of our dreams, so why don't we do it? What's missing? What is the "X Factor" that makes some people get out of their comfortable chairs, venture into unknown territory, deal with nerves and doubts and put themselves in a position to pursue their dreams? Why do most of us only talk about that but never do it?

I'll say this: if you have wondered the same thing, you're probably not going to find the answer among the skyscraper-high stacks of personal-development books on the market. I know; I've read a lot of them. Most offer similar versions of the same rewarmed advice: set goals, find your passions, make lists, think positive, make yourself accountable, etc. But if that's such wonderful advice, why do Americans spend $550 million a year on self-help books (according to MarketData Enterprises) yet struggle to implement it? Perhaps the hard reality is that many self-help gurus don't really want to put themselves out of business and have their readers or audiences resolve their own issues, shift their lives, and enjoy the life of their dreams like I do.

That is not my mission. As the book's title says, my mission is to empower dreamers to become achievers. My job is to help my readers and audiences think differently about themselves, their lives and their potential. It's my objective to help *you* find that X Factor that will motivate you and provide the spark needed for you to become one of the people who *do* face their fears, *do* make meaningful changes in their lives, and *do* attain their cherished dreams. It's possible. People do it every day, as you'll see from the lessons and real life stories I'll share with you. I believe after reading this book you will do it as well!

The Mission

You fundamentally change your life when you are willing to get uncomfortable and expand your customary ways of thinking. Affirmations and multi-step action plans are wonderful tools in theory, but they fail because they masquerade as action. Don't be fooled. Making a list is not the same as acting. The reason that so many of us struggle to realize the desired dreams for our lives is because we confuse "planning" with "doing". "Doing" is hard work. It's frightening. It can alienate people we care about. But it is the only panacea for living without the dreaded "could have-should have-would have" regret syndrome that actually works.

My mission with this book is straightforward: make meaningful action inevitable. Doing things differently than you have always done them—changing the people you hang with, going back to school, getting in shape—is uncomfortable and difficult. As a result, we have the right intentions but the wrong plan to force sustainable action that delivers results. That's why, according to StatisticBrain.com, of the 45 million Americans who make New Year's resolutions each year, only eight percent keep them.

The problem is not you; the problem is your approach. If you say to yourself, "This is the year I finally get back in shape," you are not doing anything to adjust your *mentality*—the patterns of thinking and feeling that contributed to you getting out of shape in the first place. Unless you change those, it's probably not long until the rationalizations and excuses start and before long another year has passed and you're no closer to your goal.

I'm going to demonstrate how to modify the way you think and what you feel so that you can't *not* reach your dreams. When your heart and mind are rightfully aligned, meaningful sustainable action is inevitable. Further, the urge to take action is so compelling that it dismisses fear and discomfort. The truth about motivation is that wanting something is not enough. Motivation means incubating your thoughts and emotions in a place where you have *no choice* but to do something. That's all it takes sometimes. Doing something. *Anything*. Get moving in a direction, even if it turns out to be the wrong one. There is magic in motion and unequivocally proving to yourself that you can do this. That is my gift to you with this book.

How to Read It and Who It Is For
The book has been designed to follow a process that I believe is most effective at opening minds, opening hearts and freeing the emotions that get people motivated. To help you understand and apply the processes, I have divided the book into three sections:

1. **How to Get Moving.** These three chapters are all about tapping into the powerful emotions that are the secret to becoming fiercely motivated. Human beings are conditioned to crave comfort and familiarity, so we'll often choose to stay in a negative situation (a depressive work environment, for example) because it's more comfortable than attempting to find something better. These chapters are about challenging that mindset, getting comfortable with being uncomfortable, and discovering one of the most potent motivating forces available to all of us.

2. **The Three Ps Methodology.** These chapters are all about process, putting in place a series of repeatable actions that yield desirable results. *Possible* examines your dreams and self-talk, your ability to imagine a better life and believe that you deserve it. *Probable* examines what is required to give your vision the best odds of coming true. Hint: it's all about hard work and discipline. *Predictable* looks at preparation and accountability—doing the right things over and over before breakthrough opportunities present themselves...without worrying about results.

3. **The Final Pieces.** This final section wraps things up with some incredible concepts that you may have never explored. We will talk about the idea that the story you tell others—and yourself—about

your life to date has everything to do with how you view yourself and what you think you are capable of. We'll examine the meaning of the book's title, "Empowering Dreamers To Become Achievers." Basically, daring, brave and original dreams always encounter doubt and opposition, and that's what you should aspire to attract. Finally, we'll talk about the virtue and value of simply taking action, even if you feel it might be premature.

As you read, you will also encounter tools designed to assist you in connecting with your emotions and changing how you think: worksheets, sidebars, leading questions, introspective journaling, inspirational real-life stories and more. As you read, I encourage you to complete all of these interactive elements and take notes. Feel free to skip around to material that inspires you most based on where you are in the pursuit of your dreams. I think every part of the book has value for readers, but I'm biased. If you need Part Two more than you need Part One, skip to Part Two. Make the book work for your unique circumstances.

Who can this book work for? Anyone, really. I believe the vast majority of us desire to live our best lives and become our best selves, no matter where we are today. That has certainly proven true in my speaking engagements. However, I really wrote this book with two audiences in mind:

- First, young people with the majority of their lives in front of them. They dream about becoming great and accomplishing the extraordinary. Many have been told to dream since they were toddlers but often end up deflated because no one has taught them that dreams aren't enough if you don't know how to make them come true. They lack access and exposure. It is my hope that my insights will help change this generation by empowering one young dreamer at a time.

    My heart especially goes out to young people from disadvantaged backgrounds. There is so much pessimism and cynicism swirling around these young folks, who have grown up around poverty, abuse, violence and neglect. Yet somehow, they *still* possess so much hope and potential. If you're from such a background, I want you to know your background has equipped you with a resilient spirit. I want you to know that things can get better. I believe this book can help you find your power, a power that's greater than you may realize.

- Second, mature men and women looking to reconnect with the lives they once wanted. I speak to plenty of audiences of middle-aged professionals and many seem to share a common condition: they have lost touch with the people they once thought they would become and are looking around wondering, "What happened?" If you're in that group, I'll remind you that your dreams are easily revived. They are perched right below the surface of your life, like tulip bulbs. It takes courage and some discomfort to revive them again, but it can happen.

Reclaim Your Story

But really, it does not matter if you fall into one of these two groups. Wherever you come from, wherever you are in your life, you have a story that you're writing every day. And while it may not feel like it sometimes, you are in control of where that story takes you. You can allow yourself to be defined by the circumstances of your past, or you can take control of your story and write each new chapter with conviction, courage, and confidence. I believe this book will encourage you to never stop believing, never stop achieving, and to keep on dreaming!

This is not shallow self-help talk. Every month, people in my speaking audiences remind me that we're all capable of transcending terrible hardships and fears to transform our lives. It happens more often than you might realize. People do aspire to something more. They do get past their anxieties and self-doubts. They do put their pasts behind them. They do change the world, sometimes just for themselves and sometimes for millions. They do reach goals that, not long before, seemed completely out of reach. Every day, men and women facing obstacles as daunting as yours reclaim their lives and realize their dreams.

What separates you from them? Nothing more than how you think. Change your mind and you change everything. Ready to find out how?

Ramsey Jay, Jr.
Los Angeles, California

PART ONE—HOW TO GET MOVING

CHAPTER 1

Get Comfortable With Being Uncomfortable

"The truth is that our finest moments are most likely to occur when we are feeling deeply uncomfortable, unhappy, or unfulfilled. For it is only in such moments, propelled by our discomfort, that we are likely to step out of our ruts and start searching for different ways or truer answers."

—M. Scott Peck

When I arrived at Dartmouth to begin my graduate studies, I wanted to get involved in campus life and student organizations. But because I believe in getting comfortable with being uncomfortable, I didn't want to join just any organization. So one of the first clubs I joined was the Asia Business Club.

No, that is not a typo. Like the majority of student organizations, this was an inclusive membership group. This meant you didn't have to be Asian to join, just interested in Asian business and in networking with others who had an affinity for Asian affairs, which I did. Of course, I knew what I was doing. I suspected that I would be one of the few non-Asian students in the club, and I was right. But I also figured the experience would challenge some of my preconceived thinking and open my eyes about Asian culture, business and people. I ended up being correct on all three counts. It was a terrific growth experience. I was proud to become an asset to the group, and they certainly became an asset for me.

Deliberately seeking out discomfort is not something human beings do, by and large. We are programmed to seek out the safe and familiar—to congregate with others cut from the same cloth, so to speak. From the perspective of evolution, this makes sense. In our pre-agrarian, hunter-gatherer days the only safety was found in the community. Outsiders typically did not survive. It makes sense that today, after an eye blink in an evolutionary timeframe, we still do the same thing. Goths flock to Goths, Mormons to Mormons, and African-American business students to African-American business students; we typically congregate with people from the same background. But constantly sticking with people just like us, in situations where we are perfectly comfortable, actually stymies growth.

Bodybuilders will tell you cannot stimulate muscle growth by doing the same exercises month after month. You have to switch and try new exercises, various weights, more reps or different machines in order to continually stress your muscles in dynamic ways. Muscles only grow when they're recovering from the stress and discomfort inflicted by a hard workout, not from endless repetition of the same moves. If your muscles get too comfortable with your workout routine, there is no stress, and that means no growth.

Our minds and characters are the same way. We only discover new abilities, overcome fears, create things of extraordinary value and experience real fulfillment when we are out on the edge, stretching ourselves outside of that zone of familiarity and comfort. That's when we find out how much resilience and commitment we have. By expanding our comfort zone we also turn other people into fans and unearth new capacities of mind and body.

It's our fear of venturing into the unfamiliar, then, that's holding us back from real, lasting change in our lives. We know *what* do to, but we cannot seem to *do* it. Most individuals never do more than talk about taking their lives in a new direction because the inertia of the familiar has a narcotic effect. It's soothing and comforting, but it is really what I call the *anesthesia of comfort*. You settle into a routine that's unsatisfying but undemanding, talk about all the things you're going to change, procrastinate and never do them, and before you know it you're asleep. When you finally come out of the anesthetic fog, years and countless opportunities have passed you by.

The single greatest challenge in personal development is not knowing what to do, but *getting started*. It's breaking the velvet shackles of that affable inertia and stepping into uncharted territory. That is difficult, to be sure, but it is also the only reliable way you will ever bring real, meaningful, permanent change into your career, relationships and life. As Albert Einstein said, "No problem can be solved from the same level of consciousness that created it." You have to change things. You have to discover a way to get yourself moving. It does not matter how; motivation is morally neutral. All that matters is that you act. Let me share a story about a leader who was willing to change things and act.

A few years ago, I produced and hosted a "Conversation on Leadership," featuring Les Biller. Les is the retired Vice Chairman of Wells Fargo Bank and today, along with his wife Sheri, is co-founder of the Sheri & Les Biller Family Foundation, which focuses on public education, supportive care, theatre enrichment, and career pathways. It was humbling to interview a respected leader, devoted family man and compassionate philanthropist. As I reflect on the evening, it was more than a conversational interview; it was a demystifying discourse that invited an audience to appreciate an authentic and humanizing view of an extraordinarily successful human journey.

Les shared several life lessons during our conversation, but one was truly poignant. Early in his career, Les spent a decade overseas in Italy and England, in positions of increasing responsibility. He embraced the relocation and committed to immersing himself in this exciting endeavor; as a young banker, he relished the opportunity to learn the fundamentals of the banking business while simultaneously experiencing foreign cultures. Specifically, his first assignment was working in Milan for the Italian subsidiary of a U.S. headquartered bank. Les knew that to succeed at the level he envisioned, the bank had to be managed as an Italian-centric operation. Further, he recognized that he had to foster a sincere sense of community by both living and working with his Italian colleagues and banking clientele. In fact, Les and his family were the only expats who lived in their neighborhood. This enabled him to develop genuine relationships while gaining an intimate understanding of the lifestyle and culture of his new home.

Professionally, he furthered that sense of community by investing the time getting to know his Italian colleagues. Specifically, when Les started there were 52 employees in the Italian subsidiary. By the time he transitioned to his next assignment, that number had grown to 206. Les made it a point to learn not only their names but also something personal about all 206 of his colleagues. This disciplined practice of relationship building helped him establish the foundation for his outstanding career.

As Les reflected on a career that culminated with his retirement as Vice Chairman of Wells Fargo, he insisted that his decade overseas was critical to developing both his banking acumen and his appreciation for building relationships with peers and colleagues alike. I have witnessed Les taking a down-to-earth, sincere interest in everyone he meets, whether it is an ambitious college student or a fellow C-suite executive.

To quote Les, "Do things that are fun, things that stretch you, things you love; when you love something, you will do it well." I could not agree more. I implore you to save this nugget of wisdom in your treasure chest of inspiration. Good things are bound to happen when you challenge yourself to embrace a new adventure while pursuing something you are passionate about.

Waking Up

It's not easy to wake yourself from complacency. To do so you have to purposefully shock your system: internalize the facts about the life you are living now: life expectancy, spiritual walk, salary expectation if you do not graduate from high school. The hard facts embedded in this reality check will provide the jolt you need to get moving and make changes.

Chase the Dream Or Validate the Statistic

Often, the greatest challenge is believing that legitimate change is even possible. For example, I speak to young people in a myriad of communities around the country. I have observed that each school district, staff, and administration faces unique challenges in trying to equip students with the skills they need to succeed. In those engagements where the obstacles are more pronounced, or resources are minimal, my main foes are often apathy, resignation and fatalism; the sense that nothing will change, so why bother trying?

To get this audience of young, jaded boys and girls motivated to listen and act on the lessons I have prepared to share, I have to make them uncomfortable. So I'll often lead with alarming statistics that hit home. For example, when I speak to high school students I will say the following: "It estimated that 25% of high school freshman will not graduate, which is the equivalent to 7,000 of you dropping out daily, or one of you dropping out every 26 seconds. Look at ten people sitting around you. Statistics suggest that in just a few years, at least two to three of you will not be here. One of them might be you."

Mutters, turning heads, and then the room inevitably goes silent. They are taking it in. They know the inherent truth in my statement; it is the harsh reality for our youth living in some of America's under-resourced communities. More specifically, according to a 2013 report by the Sentencing Project, approximately one in three African-American males, one in six Latinos, and one in 17 White males born can expect to spend time in prison during their life if current incarceration trends continue. So I challenge the young men in my audience to accept the reality that the decisions they make as students will either keep them on the pathway to their dreams or merely validate the disturbing statistics.

When I say these things, I can see the change in their eyes: young kids so full of hope and promise, suddenly challenged to stop and ask a hard question as they look around the room and quietly wonder, "Which ones will become a statistic? Will I become a statistic?" Tears are common, particularly when they're forced to ask which group they see themselves belonging to.

However, after this they are more receptive to what I have to say. Fear and discomfort crack the shell of complacency and denial that blinds us to where we are and what we need to do. In other words, to prepare my young audiences to understand the necessity of taking real-time action, I first have to make them confront the uncomfortable possible outcomes if they don't take full control of their lives. Like many of us, their vision of *what can be* is clouded by *what is* or *what has been*. They are skeptical that anything will ever change. That is human nature. We delude ourselves into believing that real change is hard to come by.

But change happens constantly. The Berlin Wall falls after standing for 28 years. The Boston Red Sox win the World Series after 86 years of failure. Neil Armstrong becomes the first man to walk on the moon eight years after President John F. Kennedy laid out such an ambitious dream. And young students rise up all over the country and categorically decide that they will chase their dreams despite the odds. Most inspiring, they go on to set the pace for a generation! I see it every time I am blessed to take the podium. Every day, things that seemed like they could never change *do* change.

The purpose of getting uncomfortable is to consciously seek encounters that force you to shift your habitual mindset so you can see—and accept—that not only is change possible, but that *you* can ignite it on your own. Stepping out of your comfort zone, taking risks, and venturing into the unknown is about realizing that you have the capacity and character to do things you never thought you could. This book is for people who are ready to do just that.

Three Steps to Action
In my speaking engagements and small group teaching sessions, it has become evident to me that desire is not enough to spark action. We can want things to be different with all our might, but wishing does not equal action. We need a catalyst.

That catalyst is *emotion*. Everything starts there, and for many of us that is hard to believe. We prefer to see ourselves as rational beings who carefully reason out every decision based on data. But we aren't rational—at least not entirely. If we were, we would have no trouble motivating ourselves to enact the changes we desire. The rational reasons to get in shape or start your own business are just that strong and obvious. But only a small percentage of us ever manage lasting, radical self-revision, and it's for the simplest of reasons: *profound personal change always begins with strong emotion*. ALWAYS. You can have reasons laid out in front of you from here to there and back again, but nothing will happen until emotion forces action.

Unconvinced? Think about men who engage in drastic weight loss and nutrition programs only after they suffer a heart attack. They were aware that carrying 75 extra pounds and maintaining a heavy diet of root beer, pizza, and ice cream would put them at risk for heart disease, so why not make changes before they end up in the Coronary Care Unit? Because in the absence of powerful emotion, it is convenient to dismiss or postpone the need for change with a flip thought of, "I'll get to it one of these days." However, when crisis strikes, those powerful emotions activate—in this case, the fear of life ending prematurely and the immediate accompanying thoughts of regret. That fear can *instantly* compel us to do things differently.

Now, imagine not needing a crisis like an illness, job loss or divorce to evoke emotions that motivate change. That is precisely what I'm going to teach you to do. Stimulating emotion does not just happen; it is derived from a tripartite process:

1. Consciously seeking out uncomfortable situations and relationships and thinking uncomfortable thoughts. Courting "constructive discomfort" will stir up...

2. Powerful emotions like the deep regret that you have not put forth your best effort in service of a goal, a fervent passion for a cause that speaks to your soul, or

the hunger to live your best life today without pretense. With those emotions revealed, you can harness them to spark transformative action by identifying a…

3. Role model. It is much easier to get started when you can emulate the life change blueprint belonging to someone who has already succeeded in doing what you desire to do. This is where emotion becomes action.

When you commit to this process, the dreaded follow-through phase (which is where most people struggle mightily) becomes virtually automatic. Even after it becomes too grueling to rise at 5 a.m. to get to the gym and work out, you'll still do it if you have an unquenchable fire in your belly for looking and feeling better—and the desire to avoid a stroke, heart attack, or diabetes.

Now let's examine the thing that's most effective at evoking that motivating emotion: *getting comfortable with being uncomfortable.*

Quote

"Move out of your comfort zone. You can only grow if you are willing to feel awkward and uncomfortable when you try something new."

— Brian Tracy

Regret Is the Worst Emotion

The legendary actress Lucille Ball said, "I'd rather regret the things I've done than regret the things I haven't done." Ms. Ball knew something most people have yet to master: you always benefit from making an honest attempt, even if you fail. We regret the things we do not do far more than the things we do. You regret breaking up with an old love from years past? Perfectly understandable, but at least you enjoyed the bliss before the breakup. When you get uncomfortable and take a risk, the possibility of failure comes with it.

However, you also create the opportunity to learn, grow, meet someone new, and discover the depth of your own resolve.

Think about this. What will the results be if you don't try? There won't be any. There will be zero progress, prolonged silence, feelings of resignation, and the reality that tomorrow will likely be as frustrating as today. If your life is not going in the direction that you want, that could become a paralyzing existence.

Most people who are not satisfied with the present position of their lives—whether they are 18 and bewildered, trying to discern life after high school, or 50 and fighting a midlife crisis—deal with a constant undercurrent of unease. Many have never had the courage to even try and make their dreams come true. The resulting regret can be so crippling that they turn to destructive crutches offering only a temporary high. The lasting high of taking control and acting to pursue your dreams is superior, and that is your destiny.

If you have been ignoring that persistent inner voice whispering, "Why haven't you ever tried?" or "You've got this," please listen to it instead. That voice is your conscience challenging you to defeat doubt by getting uncomfortable. We accumulate regrets each time we refuse to embrace discomfort. As those doubts accumulate, we end up reinforcing the sinister belief that we are incapable. But when we embrace uncomfortable situations, even if the outcomes aren't perfect, we are not regretful. We are exhilarated.

Rationally, Purposefully Uncomfortable

The "comfort zone" is a behavioral state where your activities are so routine that there is little risk or stress associated with just "doing you." That sounds nice and cozy, a steady comfort level that produces predictable results. However, research shows that generating extraordinary results requires a calculated increase in stress and anxiety. Psychologists call this state "optimal anxiety," a state where we are stressed just enough to stretch ourselves to the next level but not so stressed that we overreach or panic.

Trouble starts when we are so eager for instant results that we overreach, become too stressed to be productive, and experience major anxiety. This causes us to overreact and believe that any anxiety is dangerous, so we retreat from it. It becomes normal to default to the familiar, where anxiety is low. Before long, complacency becomes our normal.

However, there are careful, sensible ways to explore situations that will make you mentally, emotionally or physically uncomfortable. One way is by focusing on *variation* instead of *novelty*. Instead of diving headfirst into a new and unnerving activity, try approaching your existing activities differently. Use an alternative web browser. Watch a movie in a genre you have traditionally disliked. Listen to classical music instead of country. Go vegan for a month. Augment your wardrobe with bold colors you have never worn.

Sure, these are baby steps. But that's all right; you are *conditioning* yourself to stress, but not becoming overstressed, by getting *slightly* less comfortable. The key is to gradually increase your exposure to experiences that create discomfort so that you don't run for the familiar at the first sign of uneasiness. Going vegan might start with taking a vegan cooking class, followed by going to dinner at a vegan restaurant in an unfamiliar city.

Give yourself permission to take small steps. You don't successfully complete a marathon by trying to run 26.2 miles on Day One of training; you start out by walking or jogging a couple of miles a day and gradually build your stamina. You do the same thing in becoming comfortable with discomfort. Eventually, you'll come to *know* that you can handle it.

Here are some other ideas for embracing conscious discomfort in a smart, rational and incremental fashion:

- *Make quicker decisions.* Maximizing discomfort means learning to trust your gut. A great way to start is to resist overthinking and just act. Of course, every decision requires a little analysis, but if you're unaccustomed to getting out of your comfort zone it is easy to turn excessive analysis into a justification for remaining stagnant. Learn to rely on your instincts: if something feels like it may be a good idea and the downside is not catastrophic, go for it. (Exceptions to be made for BASE jumping, investing your entire retirement account in the stock market, and one that I am guilty of learning the hard way: trusting your internal body clock to be your alarm during international travel).

- *Combine large and small experiences.* Not every novel experience has to be earth-shattering. It might be thrilling to address 1,000 alumni at your college reunion, but it could also be terrifying for some. Blending large scale, intimidating experiences with some smaller, minor things is like working your chest and shoulders muscles one day and your core muscles the next. You end up with the right balance. Instead of being overridden by nerves as you take the podium for your first major address, what about doing a few local karaoke nights in advance? This is a reasonable incremental step to help you get comfortable being in front of an audience. Make a commitment to mix radical new experiences with more moderate ones to keep yourself moving forward.

- *Phone a friend.* Major breakthroughs rarely happen in isolation. Nowhere is it written that you must do this by yourself, you know. Granted, some uncomfortable initiatives will be solo acts, such as volunteering in a church ministry, going to back to school, saving money for your dream vacation, or reconnecting with a distant relative. But home making classes, fitness programs, book clubs, and similar activities can be done with a friend. Even more personal changes like trying a new hairstyle can become a group activity. In some of these endeavors there is actually safety in numbers, and while you should balance feeling *too* safe (remember the goal here is optimal anxiety), a little security blanket is warranted in the beginning.

- *Limit commitments early on.* Once you get your feet wet, you might be tempted to try a plethora of uncomfortable activities demanding long-term commitments: enrolling in a foreign language class on Monday, singing in the church choir on Tuesday, training with your marathon group on Wednesday and Friday and so on. But not all of your new experiences will go smoothly. Some will be educational failures, which is actually normal and healthy. However, if you have a lot of disastrous, super-stressful experiences, you are more likely to panic, abandon the mission and retreat to your comfort cocoon. Until you have a good idea of your stress threshold and how well you will rebound from adversity, beware of booking too many novel experiences at the same time.

- *Take a class.* Community college or extended education department courses are smart ways to stick your toe in the water. You can try things like yoga, photography, or learn web design with others along for the ride in a safe, structured, environment with minimal cost. Research courses offered in your community that are convenient for you.

- *Journal your emotions.* Engaging in uncomfortable experiences will conjure up intense emotions: fear and doubt, confidence and pride, etc. Harness the good while also refusing to allow the bad to influence your thinking. Make a commitment to chronicle what you are feeling and why. There is power in reflective writing. As time passes you will find tremendous value in being able to examine your progress, distill lessons learned, and handle similar experiences. You'll also find that your emotions are easier to understand and manage.

The Benefits of Getting Uncomfortable

If you're progressing through elementary uncomfortable experiences, eventually you will tire of taking baby steps. That is a good thing. Those baby steps are meant to be temporary. In time, you should be confident enough to move on to uncomfortable experiences that can transform your life: a new career, starting your own business, or a making good on your dream to travel the world for a year.

When you make that next leap, the benefits of getting uncomfortable really start to accrue. Living in a state of stimulating uncertainty:

- *Forces you to maximize your potential by developing underutilized abilities.* Consider Tiger Woods. In 2000 and 2001, he had two of the most dominant years in the history of professional golf, but were you aware that they occurred after tremendous early success and after his personal swing coach Butch Harmon retooled his stroke? Considering that Tiger's golf swing had already propelled him to the top of the sports world, he could have taken an "If ain't broke, don't fix it" attitude and no one would have argued with him. However, he and Harmon knew better: as good as Tiger was, they knew that the only way he could maximize his ability, and become the very best he could be, was to willingly push the envelope and explore unknown territory with his swing. The results speak for themselves as he proceeded to win eight additional major championships from 2002-2006.

    When you test yourself in areas where you do not have a track record of success, you might not become a champion, but you will likely identify talents and abilities you had no idea you possessed. That formula will prepare you to maximize your potential while becoming your best version of you.

- *Stimulates passionate emotions around new experiences.* Doing the same thing, the same way, day in and day out is boring. It smothers the natural joy and exultation that only comes from celebrating life's unexpected surprises. But when you step out freely on life's edges you rouse vivid emotions that remind you what it is like to be totally alive. As we have discussed, moving beyond your comfort zone can promote fear and anxiety, but it can also generate the delight that comes from succeeding at something new, the excitement of living without constraints, and the camaraderie of making new discoveries with like-minded friends. Intense emotion motivates but also adds spice and passion to the mix; it will keep you exploring new, uncomfortable experiences with a vibrant spirit of optimism.

- *Equips you with a practical skills toolbox.* The more new things you attempt, the more new skills you will learn. Even if you try out for the band and wind up getting cut, for example, you will learn something about composing arrangements, vocal production, and harmonization. Let me rephrase this in investing terms: when you invest your time in *off-comfort* activities, new skills, expanded knowledge, and increased self-confidence will be your *minimum* ROI (return on investment). You might also discover a skill set or vocation that will set the course for your whole life.

- *Helps you develop poise and adaptability.* In his superb book, *Life Of Pi*, Yann Martel writes, "All living things contain a measure of madness that moves them in strange, sometimes inexplicable ways. This madness can be saving; it is part and parcel of the ability to adapt. Without it, no species would survive." The ability to stay poised and adapt to unpredictable and stressful situations is critical to world travelers, entrepreneurs, and all of us willing to pursue our dreams. If that describes you or the person you are striving to become, then dive into discomfort. By doing so you will develop the ability to remain calm when plans change or conditions deteriorate. You'll also put yourself in a position to capitalize on the advantages that adaptability affords you over those who are inflexible.

- *Exposes you to dissimilar people and foreign environments.* We tend to congregate with others cut from the same cloth. This myopic immersion often blinds us to personal insights that we can only get from spending time with people unlike ourselves who have had different experiences.

- *Fosters self-efficacy.* One of the most serious challenges plaguing disadvantages youths is self-doubt, the belief that they do not possess enough talent to matriculate to the next level, where their dreams reside. If you suffer from the same doubt, take an intentional stroll out of your comfort zone. By doing so you will uncover new levels of self-efficacy, the belief that you are resilient and capable enough to triumph no matter what obstacles litter the road ahead. Until you give yourself approval to get knocked down, you will not comprehend how valuable your ability to get back up is. We tend to be at our best when uncomfortable and striving, overcoming obstacles and adversity. Now with that understanding, get yourself knocked down!

- *Eliminates complacency.* When you are mired in sameness and feel stagnant, you can stop caring. You can be brainwashed into believing that nothing matters, so why bother trying to change anything? Trust me when I say, it may only take a few walks on the semi-wild side and a little optimal anxiety to pivot your perspective 180 degrees. You realize that things do matter, life can change, and that you can make a difference. Discomfort is a miracle cure for chronic complacency and indifference.

Think about the wonders of travel. Specifically, think of someone whose sole annual vacation is always to the same Hawaiian beachside enclave. They stay at the same hotel, eat at the same restaurants, and see the same people. That's a missed opportunity for "optimal anxiety." Wouldn't it be special to allow a portion of your travel to be a transformative experience? It certainly is for the people I know who have decamped for the far corners of the world with nothing more than a backpack on their back. They knew no one and did not speak the local language, so they adapted. They used their instincts. They were forced to perfect skills they didn't know they had. And they came back changed for the better.

Bottom line, when you get out of your comfort zone there is no limit to what parts of you and your life that can be improved.

Shots Of Wisdom

Everything is impossible until you try and succeed. After you conquer your fear and try, you also understand that you are more capable than you realized. You will appreciate that nobody expects you to be perfect. Moreover, you find that people respect and admire those who live boldly and courageously chase their dreams. They hire them, listen to them, and want to learn how to be like them.

Who Do You Think You Are?

Venturing into the uncomfortable is not always popular with other people. Truthfully, that is one of the most common reasons motivated people offer for not trying the unfamiliar: fear that others will render judgment, be offended or disapprove. This is a popular excuse I hear often: "My friends will think that I believe I'm better than they are." Others worry that people they know will feel like they are being critiqued and become sensitive or self-conscious. For others, the prevailing fear of being ostracized from the "in" social circle takes hold.

First of all, if a friend rejects you because you have decided to live a more courageous life and chase your dreams, you might want to reconsider the true merits of that friendship. Indeed, some people will be offended when you discard routine and apathy and try something new. The fact that you are in the business of *doing* can cause them to regret their own inaction. Expect to hear questions like, "Just who do you think you are?"

Here is your answer, guaranteed not to offend but to—just maybe—make the questioner think: "That's what I'm trying to figure out." Even armed with that truthful response, you will contend with hurt feelings, offended propriety and plenty of questions whenever you trespass over traditional boundaries. Accept them all as evidence that you are on the right path.

When I joined the Asian Business Club, I did not run into angry questions. To the contrary, I was fully embraced to the point that it actually made me question the identity I projected to the club. At one of the first meetings, the club president said, "We're looking forward to a great year, and we're really excited to have a tremendous expert in networking and relationship building in our club."

Now, Asian students hail from a culture that tends to respect self-effacement and being reserved in their communication style. However, upon enrolling in a top American business school they have to adopt a more "survival of the fittest" mentality. If you want to participate in an activity or meet with a particular person, you'd better raise your hand and speak up. Because of the challenges in adapting to this new culture, at times Asian students could mistakenly be viewed as uninterested in advancement or lacking a fire in the belly.

Now we had a club member who was going to help Asian students and other members break that mold. I was thinking, "Wow, I can't wait to meet this guy!" Yes, you're already ahead of me. I was the club member the president was talking about, the networking and relationship expert!

Later in the semester, I presented my *first* official networking and relationship building workshop for my classmates and fellow club members. Subsequently, I have delivered variations of that workshop for students and young professionals all over the country. But before I delivered that first workshop, I questioned whether I was qualified, had principles that would be helpful, and was an imposter. But then I had an epiphany:

When you venture outside your comfort zone,
you're going to be nervous and feel unsure in the beginning.

The key words are "*in the beginning.*" However, when you persist, those feelings will pass. The key is to refrain from resting on your laurels when they do, keep the momentum and pledge to do something else that makes you feel as nervous and rubber-legged as a newborn fawn. Clueless about how to execute the next uncomfortable endeavor? That's promising. I believe in certain context, ignorance is an asset. If you are too smart and always have it all figured out, you can actually eliminate the opportunity to spontaneously try something because you did not know any better.

Many times in my life, I did not know that taking a certain action was a violation of standard protocol (i.e. attending the job fair at Stanford) or that I could not approach someone under the "open door policy", so I did. "Fake it 'til you make it" is less about deception and more about giving yourself permission to discover the depths of the genius inside you. If you take yourself out of the game, how will you ever know if you can play at the next level?

Stage Fright

Stage fright is not actually stage fright; it is "before going on stage fright," the fear that you are not ready to perform at the level expected. But once you take the stage and you are in the moment, the fear subsides and you execute. So ignore the nagging voice of "before going on" fear and just get out there. Be completely committed in the moment and fear does not stand a chance. Then you can look back and declare, "Yes, I did that!"

Living With the Jitters

Being a little jittery and feeling uneasy are indicators that you are truly out of your comfort zone and experiencing the healthy stress that leads to growth. I would even go so far as to say that if you are not a little afraid or nervous when you tackle a new experience or activity, you are playing it too safe.

Let me share a personal example. Back in 2005, I partnered with 16 of my fellow Tuck MBA classmates to produce *The Frosty Jester,* a comedy show featuring Tuck students using humor to recount memorable experiences during our studies or to share an amusing view on current events. Now, while speaking is my God-given gift, and has always come naturally for me, comedy is not. But with the support of my classmates, I stepped out my comfort zone and made my comedic debut. I guarantee you that Kevin Hart's career is safe, but my witty jokes and funny spoofs were not the point. My nervousness confirmed that I was in a sweet spot for development—for discovering something new about myself and further expanding on one of my innate gifts.

Trailblazers and history's notable pioneers all mastered the principle of thriving within a constant undercurrent of unease. From Susan B. Anthony to Rosa Parks, change agents resolute in their missions to challenge the status quo had to become comfortable with terribly uncomfortable, even dangerous, circumstances. By doing so, they were able to accomplish amazing feats that changed the lives of future generations. Even President Barack Obama does his job as commander in chief under a constant barrage of scrutiny, threat, and withering criticism. How? He accepts that getting comfortable being uncomfortable comes with the presidency and approaches each day accordingly.

I am regularly hired as a speech consultant where I assist others in preparing and delivering public presentations, something that terrifies most people. When I consult, this is one of the first pieces of advice I share: "You will be successful. You may be worried and your voice may tremble at the onset, but when you are front and center in that room, 99 percent of the people in the audience are petrified to do what you are doing. You have already proven yourself to be brave to everyone you are speaking to, and they will admire your faith for doing so." That simple but true affirmation empowers them to harness the nervous energy of fear and transform it into courage.

One of the rewards for having the audacity to routinely immerse yourself in unfamiliar situations, without regard for the consequences, is becoming someone who can do it. Most people cannot. This is your competitive advantage. If you find the mettle to get uncomfortable and swim against the tide, your opportunity to ascend will come at an accelerated pace.

Just Say Yes

Personal development follows a predictable process:

1. Regularly put yourself in situations of discomfort.

2. Accept the feelings of nervousness, confusion, or fear.

3. Stay committed and experience growth.

However, results are unpredictable. That is why it is imperative that you continue to explore and venture beyond your comfortable habitat: you never know what experience will be the trigger that changes everything. You might try dozens of new activities or environments and get mostly a "Ho hum," reaction. Then the very next one transforms mediocrity into transcendence and sends your life rocketing in a whole new direction.

I will challenge you with the same challenge I give my audiences: *just say yes.* Say 'yes' to things to which you have customarily said 'no'. Cultivate a standard mentality of seeking out uncomfortable situations. Court discomfort in one area of your life, even if you enjoy comfort in another.

Another solid strategy is to select a few uncomfortable experiences that are binding and make walking away as difficult as possible, like prepaid classes. Fear is a powerful emotion; don't give it the opportunity to push you off course.

Finally, develop an insatiable appetite for mastery. Mastery means that you possess such superior knowledge or skill in a discipline that you produce excellent results by instinct. Consider a concert pianist ad-libbing an impromptu finale to Beethoven's Symphony No.3 Op.55 in E flat major Eroica. He or she doesn't plan or even think, but instead creates new music in the moment, something that's close to magic. That's marvelous, but remember that all mastery begins with incompetence, mystery and discomfort. If you are willing to remain steadfast and endure in route to achieving a dream, your discomfort will drive you to succeed. That passion will be a catalyst to the emotions that motivate change, and those catalyzing emotions are the subject of the next chapter.

Summary

-   *Getting out of your comfort zone requires you to confront challenges and stress, which in turn force you to grow.*

- *Transformative changes only occur outside your comfort zone.*

- *Sudden shock or fear can motivate change.*

- *The three-part process that stimulates change: consciously seeking discomfort and challenge, harnessing powerful emotions, and identifying role models who embody your goals.*

- *Regret is the worst emotion, and we most often regret avoiding experiences that make us uncomfortable.*

- *Being uncomfortable can be frightening, but it is also empowering and exhilarating.*

- *You can experience "optimal anxiety" if you step out of your comfort zone rationally and with a plan to control the amount of stress and fear you are exposed to.*

- *The benefits of discomfort and challenge are worth the anxiety: personal growth & self-discovery, breakthrough opportunities, maximized abilities, and lasting change.*

- *When you step over boundaries, some people will render judgment, be offended, or disapprove. Count them as evidence that you are on the right path and keep going.*

- *One of the rewards for routinely immersing yourself in uncomfortable experiences is becoming someone who possesses the courage to do it—a potent competitive advantage.*

- *The process: regularly put yourself in situations of discomfort, accept the feelings, stay committed and experience growth.*

- *Develop an insatiable appetite for mastery, to be able to produce excellent results instinctively by possessing superior knowledge or skill.*

Questions To Ponder

- *Do you honestly dream of changing your life? Why? To escape your perceived future or recapture an opportunity missed in your past?*

- *How do you manage being uncomfortable, with curiosity and courage or avoidance and anxiety?*

- *What makes you uncomfortable yet stimulates you, and why haven't you pursued it?*

- *Describe your ideal comfort zone. What immediate action can you take to inch your way of out of it slowly but consistently?*

- *What are your greatest fears and worries about trying new things that make you uncomfortable?*

- *What can you do to find the courage to overcome those fears?*

- *What can you do to approach discomfort in a rational, controlled manner?*

- *How will you confront people who may try and inhibit your new quest to seek discomfort?*

CHAPTER 2

Capitalize on Your "Booster Emotions"

*"We know too much and feel too little. At least, we feel too
little of those creative emotions from which a good life springs."*
—*Bertrand Russell*

Previously I stated that motivation is morally neutral. However, the emotions that motivate are anything but neutral. They are justifiably intense as they must be in order to shift us from Park to Drive and get us moving towards our destiny.

I call these motivating emotions "booster emotions" because they are akin to the NASA rocket boosters that launch a space shuttle into orbit: a sudden shot of extra power that breaks the grip of inertia and gets you moving in a new direction. Sometimes, these emotions can be unwelcome or alarming: fear, discomfort, or anxiety. As I mentioned in Chapter One, those are the emotions I evoke when I challenge my young audiences to realize that each day, they choose to either chase the dream or validate the statistics.

Sometimes that type of emotional jolt is necessary. It takes potent emotions to crack the shell of complacency and denial and get us to act. Whether I am speaking to youth or adults, I often have to warn them of the consequences of being lethargic. Fear, in particular, is a potent "booster emotion." As just one example, consider women and money in our culture. According to the 2014-2015 Prudential Research Study, "Financial Experience and Behaviors Among Women," 36 percent of the women surveyed say they aren't prepared to make wise financial decisions and aren't even sure what information they need to look at when weighing their options.

But when a marriage falls apart or a husband abruptly passes away, it's easy to understand why fear motivates these same women to learn everything they can about their personal and household money matters. It's a choice between becoming financially literate or permanently paralyzed and dependent because they "didn't know what they didn't know."

We have talked about the importance of getting uncomfortable in order to evoke the booster emotions that motivate change. Now, we are going to closely examine those emotions—what they are, why they work, and most importantly, how to use your own powerful emotional responses to fuel positive change in your life.

Gratitude List

If you want to tap into your well of gratitude, start by creating a Gratitude List. Write down everything you are personally grateful for: you can walk, you can talk, you can see, you have clean water, etc. I believe you will be shocked by how quickly this exercise reorients your mind on being grateful for your abundance and minimizes your ability to lament your lack. Further, once complete your Gratitude List will serve as a cherished token reminder of how incredibly blessed you are.

We Are Not Rational

The so-called "dismal science" of economics has been built on the bedrock principle of economists who believe that we are "rational actors." In other words, when presented with options, most people would choose the one that made the most sense. Confronted with a choice between going into debt to buy a brand-new $85,000 BMW and continuing to drive the older but paid-for sedan, economists insisted that most of the time a man would choose to be thrifty and keep his old sedan. Seems simple, right? But you and I both know reality is not so simple. In fact, I would be willing to bet that you were not rational actors this past year and that you made a few economic decisions that were less than rational. Am I right? It's all right; we've all done it.

Starting as far back as 1994, the rational actor model has come under intense scrutiny and lost much of its legitimacy. It's become evident that individuals, companies and governments do not always act rationally. Often people purchase items that they want but do not need because of the emotional stimulant they receive.

We are not as rational as we think we are. We make a number of decisions based on emotion and then retroactively source facts and figures to *rationalize* those decisions. Think back to the man who purchases a $85,000 BMW. He probably does so because of the emotions he experiences when thinking about the sleek design, contour and finish, the way the bucket seats fit his driving style, and of course how much he loves the way it makes him look while driving. It is only *after* he has test driven the car, and is still in the dealership showroom, that he gets on his smartphone and starts reciting all of the consumer safety reports, collision reliability studies, and fuel performance economy data to justify the purchase he has already made in his head.

When you are motivated and on the verge of making seismic changes, emotion is your powerful ally. It is something you can and should leverage to get out of the starting gate. And really it does not matter which emotions you are driven by. They could be the more welcomed emotions—love, pride, honor—or unwelcome feelings like fear, envy or regret. All that matters is that they compel you to act. Do you feel strong emotions about certain parts of your life? If so, honor and recognize them as core components of who you are.

Imagine that you are a middle-aged woman who, as an adolescent, always dreamed of becoming a concert pianist. However, as you matured life took you down an alternate course. Ultimately, you became an elementary school teacher, wife and mother. Those are admirable accomplishments, but deep down in your soul, a part of you continues to yearn for one more shot at the music career you dreamed of in your childhood. In fact, each time you walk by the local music store and see the pianos in the window, a wave of wonderment and regret causes knots to form in your stomach and your heartbeat to quicken. You then hear a whispering voice in your head: *Ignore those feelings. Don't look back. That ship has sailed.*

That is terrible advice. Your emotions are trying to tell you something, and you must listen. Insist on giving voice to those feelings and respect them. Our emotions are often a better guide to what we truly desire than our intellects. If you pay attention to them, and I believe you will, your journey to transformation will be well underway.

When you feel the powerful, almost disorienting emotions that come with getting outside your comfort zone, stop, think, and ask yourself:

What is this feeling telling me to do?

Emotions are not just the result of chemical reactions in your brain and gut. They are signposts that guide you on the pathway to a better life. However, in order to utilize them effectively you must be wise enough to discern what they are telling you, follow up and take the proper actions. Developing that acute awareness—that new dimension of perspective— takes hard work. I implore you to be disciplined and stick with it. It can change everything.

The Big Four Motivating Emotions

For additional context on how harnessing powerful emotions can help catalyze change, I would like to share a little bit about my grandmother, Mary Lee Barrett. She was a magnificent source of strength. She lived in the old South of Georgia and grew up in an era governed by racism and oppressive Jim Crow laws that forbade her from pursuing her dreams. Yet she still successfully raised ten children on her own and always encouraged me to follow my own dreams. Starting from the more enlightened launching pad of Ventura, California, I have been fortunate to do just that.

After each milestone I was blessed to achieve, I found a new dream, and my grandmother was always proud and encouraging. A few of my most cherished memories are of her traveling from Georgia to be present at my graduation from Ventura High School, California State University, Fresno, and the Tuck School of Business at Dartmouth. She was always there to see her oldest grandchild progress on his journey.

She possessed a radiant smile that lit up every heart and soul in the room. She had a voice wrapped in wisdom a result of a life well-lived. She would say to me, "Hey Ram, keep on!" Those words inspired me to fulfill my calling. I believe she lived some of her own dreams through me, and I was able to realize those dreams because of her sacrifice, encouragement and faith.

She was promoted to heaven in 2010, but her image and sincere, encouraging words have left an indelible footprint on my heart. My love for her is infinite, and in her memory, I will do my best to carry on her legacy by leaving indelible footprints on the lives of the people I am blessed to come in contact with.

My heartfelt gratitude towards my grandmother has been a potent motivator for me to keep pushing and striving. *Gratitude* is one of the four great motivating emotions. Within the context of personal growth and achievement, it is critical to understand that gratitude is more than just thankfulness. It is a fierce desire to make proud the people who believed in, supported and inspired you.

My grandmother was one of those people. My parents were, too. My mom and dad were two of my earliest role models because of their never-ending belief in my dreams along with an uncompromising work ethic. As I reminisce about my childhood, I know they both often went without so I could go *with* and underwriting those sacrifices was a never-ending belief and an uncompromising work ethic. They both continue to be loyal employees at the same employers for more than three decades. As long as I have been alive, they have been early risers, demonstrating the nobility of consistent excellence in work that, while not always glamorous, is undeniably important.

Heartfelt gratitude toward people who have sacrificed for you, inspired you, or paved the path you are now traveling, is a powerful motivating force.

It fueled my journey to earn my MBA at Dartmouth, build a career in the financial industry, establish a professional speaking platform, and write this book. I dare not constrain where God may take me next.

Now, let's become intimately familiar with the other three motivating booster emotions:

- *Fear.* You might subscribe to the adage that fear paralyzes, and in many cases that is true. However, in certain circumstances the right kind of self-invoked fear can instantly and effectively change your thinking and habits. Remember the fears of the man after his heart attack and the wife who suddenly found herself divorced and financially illiterate? Those are valid life-altering fears, but they are also the result of crises. I challenge you to be proactive in using fear in a different, more constructive way.

     I'm talking about the type of fear that you consciously evoke by thinking about the implications of real life. For instance, the fear that you will never escape your old neighborhood or never be able to give your children the life you have always wanted for them. This is the fear of never living the life you imagined or becoming the extraordinary person you always dreamed of becoming. It's the fear of externalizing those two dreadful words: "If only." This type of self-provoked fear can be an incredibly powerful emotive force to get you up, moving and experimenting.

     I am a firm believer that life only owes you one opportunity to step forward—but that if you are obedient that step can change everything in a moment! It might be an outside-the-box job offer in a new industry, a chance to travel out of the country for the first time and study abroad, a friend asking you to be their study partner while taking singing and guitar lessons, or countless other opportunities. But if you allow fear to overtake your ability to be alert and attentive, you could miss it. If you are resilient, life will likely afford you more than once chance, but what if it doesn't? That would be a tragedy. Get in the habit of posing "what if" scenarios to yourself, and seriously answer the questions while thinking about the implications:

- What if I neglect my health and wellness and suffer serious medical challenges as I age?

- What if I could have realized many of my goals if only I would have tried?

- What if I believed I was as talented as all of my teachers did?

- What if passing on pursuing my dream day after day results in me spending years daydreaming in a cubicle?

- What if I could have been a change agent for the next generation if I had just shared my story?

- What if I am called upon to spend years caring for a sick loved one?

There is nothing wrong with consciously making yourself feel the fear of what might happen if you do not change how you are living your life. Remember, when it comes to motivation, emotions are neutral. Whatever gets you moving is a good thing.

It's often said that if you do something you love, you will never work a day in your life. Nice advice, but let's agree — not always practical. However, even if you are unable to make your passion a full-time career today, if it is a genuine love I challenge you to find ways to feed that passion within your current endeavors. How can you take your passion and infuse it into your current routine?

- *Love.* Motivating love is the kind of abiding love that drives you to feel replenished while depleting yourself to serve someone or something beyond yourself: God, your spouse, your children, or your country. This kind of love converts actions and choices that seem senseless to others and makes them *make* sense. It refuses to allow you to give up no matter the odds. Abiding love makes the irrational rational and fuels impossible acts of selflessness and courage.

  Consider the single father who works three jobs so that each of his kids can be properly cared for. He is constantly exhausting himself emotionally, physically, mentally, and abandoning his own dreams, but the notion of quitting or asking his kids to settle for less *is not an option*. Why? Abiding love translates thoughts of sacrifice for you into the desire to benefit those you care about.

  Does someone or something spark that kind of love in you? Who is it? What is it and why? What would you do for the people or cause that you love? More important, is there anything that you would not do?

- *Passion.* Passion is a burning fire for something. It is that thing that you obsess over, that ignites vigorous energy in your spirit. For some, it's playing acoustic guitar or writing acrostic poetry; for others, it's abstract photography or rehabbing classic automobiles. It does not matter what your passion is as long as it is something that you hunger for.

Passion puts people in the proverbial "zone" where things seem effortless; you can work around the clock without feeling fatigued. As a former collegiate Division One track and field sprinter, there were times when I experienced that sort of "flow" where running in a 400-meter race or completing an off-season distance run was so easy that time seemed to stop. I have had the same feeling when speaking to an audience and I see them have that "aha" moment. When you are working in your optimal passion zone, you are in a state known as *unconscious competence*, where you can perform at your highest level, for what seems like an eternity, without even thinking.

Passion makes it feel as though your capacity to study, rehearse, and execute is limitless; that sensation can influence every area of your life. You are fully alive and engaged. The opposite is being cynical, bored, indifferent, and exhausted, and ultimately burning out. That is the harsh penalty of neglecting your passion. Many people do not follow their passions, allowing doubters to talk them out of the pursuit—or worse yet, abandoning it on their own out of the fear of failure. But unfulfilled passion metastasizes into crippling regret. You need to commit to keeping your passion alive!

Consider Australian triathlete Chris "Macca" McCormack. He is history's most accomplished triathlete, but his dominant career in the multi-sport discipline of swimming, biking, and running, almost never got off the ground. At 22, he was an accountant who desperately ached to pursue his passion and compete on the European triathlon circuit. However, McCormack's parents, worried that their son would not be able to support himself financially, counseled him to obtain an office job as an accountant.

He heeded their counsel but hated every second of it. With each turn of the calendar, there was a relentless gnawing in his gut that if he did not at least attempt to compete for a spot on the European team, he would live with unimaginable regret for the rest of his life. Unwilling to let the gnawing persist, McCormack resigned and *secretly* started training. The pursuit of your passion is your responsibility and may not be anyone else's business.

Each day, his father dropped him off at the train station, assuming his accountant son was going to the office. Little did Chris's father know that as soon as he left, McCormack swapped his wingtips and suit for tennis shoes, singlet and shorts, and spent the day training. At the end of the "workday", he showered, changed back into his suit, and met his father at the train station, telling him all about his exciting "day at the office." However, after determining he had kept up the facade long enough, Macca told his Dad the truth, sold his possessions, and bought a ticket to Europe to pursue his passion. This was his all-or-nothing mission. Today he is the most decorated male triathlete in history, so it was a pretty good call for him to go all in and pursue his passion.

Each of us has a passion. The question you must force yourself to answer is, *what is stopping you from pursuing yours*? Odds are, it's fear, at least in part. But there's another question to ask: "What's the worst thing that can happen if you decide to pursue your passion?"

The second question becomes even more powerful and moving after my speeches to high school students. I cannot begin to tell you how many students have told me that they are *not* going to apply to an elite college because they believe their GPA and SAT scores are inferior to those published in the college marketing guides. I ask, "Do you know how many students are accepted into those schools without those numbers, just because they applied?" I challenge them to realize if they are truly passionate about their goals, how can they give up so easily and not even submit an application? What's the worst that could happen? You can see the light come on in their eyes, and the same question applies to you.

Embrace the restlessness that keeps you awake at night. Let it fuel a fierce desire to do something about it. Then do it. If you are determined to allow your passion to live, you will find a way.

Recognition and Perspective

Feeling these powerful emotions is vital, but they are only one part of the equation. Unless you recognize the emotion for what it is and acknowledge that it requires action, it will be little more than a powerful set of physical symptoms that keep your mind racing, your gut churning, and feed a perpetual ache for something that is just out of reach. You must give voice to your most potent feelings and respect them for what they are: a voice telling you that *something must change or you will have deep regrets for the rest of your life.*

The tangible benefit of transferring emotion into action comes by following these three steps:

1. Embrace and experience the emotion.

2. Understand why you are feeling the emotion.

3. Determine action to take as a result of the emotion.

Experiencing emotions like fear or passion are easy. You don't have to do anything; they'll demand your attention. But it takes an act of will to stop and ask why you are feeling the emotion. That second step is critical, and many of us simply refuse to do it. Disgruntled people ignore their emotions because they do not want to be reminded of what the emotion is trying to tell them. Others are racing through the business of their agenda-driven life too fast to pause and acknowledge what they are feeling and why.

After more than a decade of speaking engagements the data from my audiences is unmistakably clear: most have never hit pause long enough to really explore their emotions. Moreover, when they have, it was a transactional analysis: *What do I have to do to stop feeling this way?*

That is the wrong question. Replace it with some of the following:

-   What is this emotion trying to tell me?

-   Instead of acting to silence it, how can I embrace and understand it?

-   If I do not act on this feeling, what will change?

-   If I act on this feeling, what might change?

-   Will that change bring me closer to experiencing the life I desire?

When I pose these questions to my audiences, eyebrows go up and eyes twinkle. These are questions many have never asked before, and the answers are often revelatory When a 17-year-old who sadly lost his mother to breast cancer as a child acknowledges his desire to make his single father proud of him, or when a 45-year old middle manager realizes that her depression about her job has actually been a passion for starting her own business, you can see the lights illuminating the path forward come on. There is a complete mind shift that shouts, "I must do this!" Even though they have already tried and failed, they have optimism. They have hope.

Who or what are you serving? What is your calling? What is the gift you want to share with the world? Knowing those answers can crystallize your perspective and give your emotions purpose. When I was very young, I wanted to work with money. As fate would have it, one of my first jobs was as a teller at a small community bank in the town of Santa Paula, California. ATMs were not as common then, so patrons regularly came into the branch to do their banking.

The agriculture industry is one of the largest employers in Santa Paula, and as a result, I was fortunate to find satisfaction and meaning in assisting long lines of customers, many of whom came directly to the bank to cash their checks in the afternoon after working long hours in the fields. I felt gratitude as I understood that I was actually playing a small part in helping hard working citizens put food on the table and provide for their families.

That gratitude surfaced again after I took my first Finance 101 course at Fresno State's Craig School of Business. I recall going home for the holidays and reviewing my mom's retirement account statement. I noticed that a couple of the funds were heavily weighted in dotcom stocks, advised her to keep a close eye on that and think about asking her advisor if they should rebalance her portfolio. As a result of these early experiences, I discovered that finance connected me to people's well-being, something I cared intensely about. I fell in love with what I did and its potential to help people live better and achieve their dreams.

That love was a key motivating force that helped me complete my undergraduate degree in Finance at Fresno State and my MBA. Emotion can have that same motivating power in your life. It makes things that seem senseless make sense. It turns irrational thoughts and behaviors into rational ones.

In February 2015, I had the honor of interviewing five top rising physician/ research scientists as part of my support of the Cedars-Sinai Sports Spectacular Fellowship Program. Dr. Chidinma Chima-Melton, a Pulmonary and Critical Medicine Fellow, was born in Nigeria, moved to England as a child, and ultimately completed her undergraduate degree in Computer Science and Management in London. She leveraged her undergraduate credentials to jumpstart her professional career in investment banking. However, after a couple of years she realized that was not her passion. She had very little job satisfaction and hungered for a career that would allow her to contribute more to humanity. So what did she do? She followed her emotions. During volunteer sessions at St. Luke-Roosevelt hospital in Manhattan, the big four motivating emotions of gratitude, fear, love and passion that she felt while serving patients were too strong to suppress. Furthermore, she listened when those emotions called her to explore medicine.

It didn't matter that she was a banker who knew nothing about medicine. Dr. Chima-Melton used her lunch break to Google "how to become a doctor." A couple of mouse clicks and phone calls later, she learned about the MCAT, took the exam, was accepted to Stony Brook Medical School, completed her residency at Yale, and the rest is history.

Today Dr. Chima-Melton's research focuses on Idiopathic Pulmonary Fibrosis (IPF) – a lung disease that causes hardening of the lungs, making breathing difficult. The cause of IPF is unknown but her research focuses on determining the role that immune cells called macrophages might play in the disease's progression—and may help identify a cure in the future. Just think how much different her story would have been had she not heeded her motivating emotions and remained an investment banker!

What is the voice inside you saying about the emotions that you are experiencing? Are you listening? What actions are you going to take to follow the path they are you leading you down?

Pull Up That Crab!

You may have heard of the crabs in a bucket metaphor. First, imagine a bucket full of live crabs. Now, when one attempts to escape up and over the lip of the bucket, the other crabs pull it back down, as if to say, "If I can't, you can't." That's the mentality some people will have when they see you trying to follow your dreams. But what if, instead of crabs trying to pull the ambitious crab back, he was able to reach the lip and help pull the next closest crab up with him? Everyone stands a better chance of achieving freedom than of remaining trapped. When others are trying to bring you down, why not try to inspire and elevate them and show them that they can accomplish their goals as well?

Who Told You That?

While you ponder those questions, let me pose what is termed a *self-penetrating* question. There are a few of them, and ironically, the answers are less important than the process we follow to search for those answers. That process shapes and reveals the deepest truths about how we feel about ourselves. The most important *self-penetrating* question is:

Am I worthy?

Some of us spend a lifetime seeking that answer. "Am I worthy to defy my family, my traditions or my fears and chase my dream, even when no one else believes in me?" Let me be clear. If you believe you are worthy, you are. Period. Of course, plenty of people will challenge your conviction. Few things provoke resentment like jealousy, and few things provoke jealousy like a person witnessing someone else pursue things they have never had the courage to attempt. If audacity breeds animosity, success in an audacious pursuit breeds even more of it.

In *Pulp Fiction*, Samuel L. Jackson quotes a powerful scripture, Ezekiel 25:17: "The path of the righteous man is beset on all sides by the inequities of the selfish and the tyranny of evil men." When walking in obedience to the call on your life, you will face resistance. Your choice to move beyond fears and self-imposed limitations will shine a light on others inability to do the same. Some people will mirror your emotions, reflecting them back to you in reverse. The more determined you are to pursue your passion, the harder those people will try to discourage you (some unknowingly), because they see their failure reflected in you.

Families can be obstacles to the pursuit of your passions—because they want the best for you, but also don't want to see you get hurt. Sometimes, families (especially multi-generational families) don't understand risk and reward in today's world, and don't realize that you may have to take a different path to your dreams than they took to theirs.

To combat the tendency of others to hinder your decisions, I've found two strategies to be effective. First, acknowledge the effect that outside opinions have on your confidence and identity. That is the only way you can process negative influences without losing your positive momentum. The naysayers are coming, and if you think you can march forward without encountering them, think again. The harsh reality is that as you move forward, you cannot bring everyone with you. Knowing that you cannot avoid the detractors helps you prepare to withstand their words with your determination intact.

Second, when someone tells you that you can't do something or that your dream is impossible, ask them, "Who told you that?" Put them on the spot—respectfully but firmly—and challenge the source of their insight about *your* abilities. I have used this technique for years and every time, the only source for their data is in their heads. Odds are, you will discover the same. Remember, defeatist talk reflects someone else's insecurity, not your inability.

The higher you rise, the more you should be prepared to protect your mind from the influence of others—to filter both their positive and negative opinions. Growing up, I had to do just that. When I was a child, I knew that God had not granted me special gifts with the goal of me becoming just another average person. As I developed my speaking, athletic, leadership, financial, and academic abilities, I would periodically hear people asking questions like, "Do you think you're better than me?" "Have you forgotten where you came from?" and "Who do you think you are?"

I was called a kiss-up, teacher's pet, and even a sell-out. I blocked it out as best an adolescent boy could. However, I was also aware that if I was going to do extraordinary things with my gifts, I could not have ordinary goals or ordinary standards.

Asking, "Who told you that?" forces the naysayer to confront their flip attitude and question their authority to judge your prospects. Confront them and naysayers will cower, unable to articulate any substantive reasons to doubt you. This is a *powerful* tool in your arsenal. It puts authority back in your hands. I receive correspondences from people of all ages who have challenged their detractors by asking this powerful question. I encourage you to do the same.

Hit Singles Often and Consistently

Detractors frequently insist that major life changes are not practical. Their rhetoric is full of negative prefaces: You can't…You don't…No one from here…How can you… *You can't apply for membership given your background. You don't have the money to start your own business. No one from here has ever run for a political office. How can you consider going back to school when you have a family to support?* And so on.

Take a moment and think of the negative prefaces you have heard. Now, it's true that what you are passionate about may not be practical immediately. But those negative sentiments, combined with your own fears, can make you feel like burying your head in the sand. Maybe there are legitimate reasons to postpone your dream; that does not mean it's dead! If you can't hit a home run today, you keep that dream alive and find ways to hit singles—to keep moving forward.

Learning to trust where your emotions are leading you is a transformational habit. The more often you permit your feelings to propel you toward change—even if it means hitting a single, like attending a seminar on starting your own business before you quit your job or running a 5K instead of a marathon—the more comfortable you will get at jumping at opportunities and trusting your instincts. Before long, chasing your passion and confronting your fears will become as natural as breathing.

That habit is crucial, because overnight success is a myth. Real, sustained change—the kind that transforms not only your circumstances but your character—takes time. You have to show up, lift the weights, make the sales calls, write the chapters, study the curriculum, save the money, etc., and keep hitting singles by pounding out small wins day after day. Do those little things consistently over time and those wins begin to accumulate. Eventually, they become big victories: the thriving start-up company, the produced screenplay, the graduate degree, the money to travel the world with your family.

Success comes more often when you hit singles consistently; home runs are rare. Keep in mind that an enormous swing may result in a home run, but it will also increase the likelihood of a strikeout. Over time, taking smart, incremental risks repeatedly will lead to success you can believe in. In other words, to change your life you do not have to carelessly jump off a bridge…but you do have to jump.

Embrace your booster emotions: fear, gratitude, love and passion. What are they telling you that you simply *must* do? Follow where they lead. If you experience a bit of adversity, double down on your efforts. Do not fear adversity; it is a feature, not a bug. Adversity stretches you while it tests you. It is also an indicator that you are on the right track. If you were safe and comfortable, you would not be maximizing your opportunity to chase your dreams.

Every person who has enjoyed multiple seasons of success did so by learning and rebounding from adversity in a healthy way. Adversity is the crucible that changes you, that makes you stronger and wiser. There is no way to have sustained success without the ability to manage adversity well.

When things get unnerving, which they will, remember you do not need all the answers at this stage. All you have to do is to act on your commitment to take action. When you are in need of guidance, find someone who has already done what your emotions are urging you to do. That someone is your role model, and the focus of our next chapter.

Summary

- *Motivation is a morally neutral force.*

- *Emotions are the most powerful motivators. Most people make radical changes not for rational reasons but because emotions leave them no choice.*

- *The big four motivating emotions are gratitude, fear, love and passion.*

- *The three stages in using these "booster emotions" to motivate you are embracing and experiencing the emotion, understanding why you are feeling the emotion, and determining what action will satisfy the emotion.*

- *Emotion makes actions that seem senseless make sense.*

- *When you decide to escape your current circumstances, some people will resent you and try to drag you down.*

- *When someone tells you, "You can't do that," an authoritative response of, "Who told you that?" gives you back your power.*

- *Trusting and obeying your emotions is a transformational habit.*

- *Ultimately, hitting singles consistently leads to success.*

Questions To Ponder

- *Which of the four booster emotions do you feel in your life daily and why?*

- *What do you think that emotion is trying to tell you to do?*

- *What has made you reluctant to find out where acting on that emotion might take you?*

- *What is the worst thing that can happen if you act on the emotion?*

- *What can you do today to begin moving towards where that feeling is leading you?*

- *What are the practical obstacles (money, time, work, family commitments, etc.) that might stop you from exploring new options and how can you mitigate them?*

- *Can you list ten "singles"—small wins—that will move you towards your ultimate goal without being too disruptive to your life right now?*

CHAPTER 3

Identify Your Role Model

"To help the young soul, to add energy, inspire hope, and blow the coals into a useful flame; to redeem defeat by new thought and firm action, this, though not easy, is the work of divine men."

—*Ralph Waldo Emerson*

In Chapter Two, I shared memories of my grandmother and her perseverance during the oppression of the Jim Crow era, along with those of my mother's and father's sacrifices in order to afford me the opportunity to chase my dreams. The deep gratitude created by those memories inspired me to develop what I believe to be the most powerful motivational tool in my arsenal. Now, I want it to become yours. I call it the "Quintessential Motivator", or QM.

Near the conclusion of my speaking engagements or leadership workshops, I introduce the QM. I request five minutes of absolute silence and ask everyone in the building to close their eyes. I wait until the entire room is almost uncomfortably still and quiet, and then I declare that I am preparing to impart the most valuable gift I can offer.

"In your mind," I say, "I want you to isolate the one person in your life who is most responsible for you being where you are right now," I say. "You might not be where you want to be, but you also aren't where you could have been because of this person."

I let them meditate on this for a few minutes and then say, "Now, go deeper and deeper into this person. What do they look like? How do they dress? How do they talk? Burn this person's image into your mind in such clarity and detail that they can never be erased. Replay every second of the uplifting voice mails they left, reread the inspiring words they wrote to you. Think about the feeling you had when the text message "I love u" appeared on your phone when you really needed it. Even when you were consumed with all of your own stuff, think about how this person kept calling, kept reaching out, kept encouraging, and kept believing in you."

By this time an atmosphere of communion has formed and the audience is deeply emotional. I give them a few more minutes to reflect on *who* this person is in their life, *what* specific things they did to support them, and then I really drive it home.

"This is the person who never gave up on you," I say. "The person who selflessly sacrificed their wants and needs to ensure that yours were served first. Now, it may not happen today, but at some point, be it here or in heaven, you will come face-to-face with that person, and you will be asked the question: 'How did you do? How did you do with all the love? How did you do with all the sacrifices I made for you? How did you with all the gifts I gave you? How did you do?'"

By now, most of the audience is in tears. I then tell them that there are only two answers to the "How did you do?" question. One starts with, "Well…" and meanders through a series of qualifiers and rationalizations that culminate in the person failing to reach his or her potential.

Then I tell them the second answer. "That answer is, '*I finished the race.* It may not have been pretty, and I may not have been first, but everything you put into me, I exhausted. And every time I felt like I didn't have enough to keep on and was on the verge of quitting, I thought about you. When I thought about you and imagined where I would be if you would have ever given up on me, I knew that I had to finish the race. And that is exactly what I did!'"

After that last statement, I ask my audience to open their eyes. I challenge them to make a personal and binding commitment to their QM at that moment: no matter what obstacles lie on the path between them and their dreams, they will *finish the race.* There is something intrinsically powerful in this; it gives you a level of credibility and authenticity to be able to empower others to do the same.

As I close the QM exercise, I tell my audiences that if they take nothing else away from their time with me, I know they will never forget the images, sounds, and feelings of those five minutes when they connected with their QM.

Each of our races is unique, but we share a common desire: the desire to live tomorrow the life we dream of today. In order to make that happen, we must have a motivational tool to lean on to ensure that we *finish the race.* The QM is that tool. Consider it a key implement in your personal arsenal as well.

What Is a Role Model?

The QM works anywhere, on any audience, because it is authentic but extremely private. Each person's unfiltered thoughts, and the resulting emotions, are between them and their QM. I'm not "workshopping" them, nor are they feeling any peer pressure. This encourages their full participation and uncensored vulnerability without the fear of any social repercussions.

In fact, people regularly, voluntarily and spontaneously open up to their fellow audience members, share intimate stories, and pay moving tributes to their QM. Picture one person after another standing up and saying, "I'd like to share why my QM is so important to me." To me, the climax comes when many attendees make public declarations and binding commitments before witnesses by saying, "In honor of my QM, I make a commitment to finish the race no matter what!" It is miraculous.

The QM resonates with people in a profound way. People constantly tell me that my presentation was the first time they ever thought about their QM in that manner. Several have shared that they left my presentation and immediately sought this person out—even if they had been out of contact for a decade or more. The QM exercise is particularly moving in multigenerational audiences with students and their parents present. Observing students thinking about their parents, while the students' parents are thinking about *their* parents or beloved mentors, is dynamic and powerful. Both groups share such intimate testimonies with each other.

However, the most beneficial attribute of the QM exercise is that it *never* expires. It is available wherever and whenever it is needed—and often that's when we are struggling and feeling isolated.

Another key reason the Quintessential Motivator is so effective is that it places tremendous value on the idea of a *role model* and the role model's place in answering that critical question, "Am I worthy?" Every single one of us wants to be defined as worthy, and no opinion is more valuable than that of someone who knows every step of the journey we have walked because they have done it, or has sacrificed mightily in order that we might walk it. Quite simply, a role model is:

Someone who shows you the way by living the right way.

Let me dispel a couple of myths about role models. Number one, you do not need to know your role model personally. Number two, your role model does not need to have experience in the endeavor you're dreaming about. But your role model *should* be someone who has faced obstacles similar to those you anticipate encountering, and triumphed over them. It could be a parent or grandparent, a celebrity or CEO, a military general or one of history's great political activists whose story touched you.

You Are Worthy

People often sheepishly asking me questions like this, "Who am I to be contacting such a highly accomplished, successful person as my role model?" Who are you? You are a leader of the future if you self-appoint yourself as one. You ARE that potential role model writ small. Everyone had to start somewhere, and no one makes it anywhere without guidance and support. Thus, you should never assume that your present seat makes you unworthy to reach out to someone of influence. They just might take an interest in you and change your life by serving as a human bridge to a breakthrough opportunity.

As you begin to act on the motivating power of your emotions, a role model is essential to reduce the natural bewilderment you'll feel while trying to navigate territory that's outside of your comfort zone. It's normal to find yourself scratching your head and wondering, "What do I do now?" That being the case, resist the temptation to reinvent the wheel to discover the answer.

Now is the time to be more calculated, methodical, and strategic. There is no virtue in toiling on the hamster wheel, experiencing mistake after mistake, without gaining traction just so you can make like Frank Sinatra and trumpet that 'you did it your way'. Instead, identify your role model, study their best practices, and make their strategy work for you just as it did for them!

Therein lies the practical magic of role models: they provide proven strategies for proceeding down the path to your dreams. And as I wrote earlier, you don't need to know your role model personally to emulate him or her. A role model is a tangible inspiration whose life proves that your aspirations are more than reasonable. For example, when aspiring young entrepreneurs approach me after a workshop and share that they have a dream to develop and revitalize urban communities, I instantly counsel them to adopt Magic Johnson as a role model. It doesn't matter if they personally know him; odds are, they do not. However, they certainly have permission to emulate his success model by studying his work.

After Magic retired from his Hall of Fame basketball career, he embarked on building a business empire whose portfolio has included Urban Coffee Opportunities (a joint venture with Starbucks), Magic Johnson Theaters (a nationwide chain of movie theaters), 24 Hour Fitness health clubs, TGIF Friday restaurants and other corporate joint ventures predominantly focused on serving underserved communities. Further, to help put Magic's business prowess into perspective, in 2015 I heard him deliver the keynote address at the opening plenary session of the NAHRO (National Association of Housing & Redevelopment Officials) National Conference, where he stressed the power of ALWAYS having a positive mindset when you dream so you can bring about positive changes in your life and community.

Magic's business acumen and optimistic mindset make him the perfect role model for these aspiring urban real estate developers, who can compress their learning curve by digesting his success blueprint and modeling him step-by-step as best they can.

Another critical benefit of having a role model is they provide a template you can follow when you fall down and need a practical strategy to help you get back up. Major directional shifts in our lives often find us on the edge of defeat. When we have been besieged by misfortune, poor health, natural disasters, or financial hardships, we have a binary decision to make: get up or stay down?

Truth: at some point, we all receive one more rejection or setback than we believe we can tolerate. You get a denial from that surefire opportunity you were confident was going to validate your hard work and sacrifice. Yet despite suffering another crippling defeat, some of us find the resolve to press forward. Those who do are usually able to find strength from their role models and say, "She had every reason to quit, yet she persevered and kept moving forward."

Your role model absorbed the same kind of knock-down blow (notice "down" not "out") that you experienced, took a knee, and just as the count neared ten, rose to their feet, fought back, and ultimately triumphed. Knowing that can provide the sustaining fuel you need to refuse to give up.

Change Is Not a Do-It-Yourself (DIY) Project
Your role model is the answer to the most arduous question in personal development:

How do I get beyond intention and take purposeful action?

Think of how many people have absolute clarity on where they want to go and possess the passion and energy to make it happen. Yet they remain painfully stagnant. Even when you are standing on point A with a clear line of sight to point B, it can still appear a million miles away. You may be uncertain about where your emotions are leading you, but even in the face of such uncertainty, you must act. Taking affirmative, decisive action, despite your uncertainty, is energizing and empowering—and it's even more so when you do not have to make the journey in solitude.

The idea of the role model ends the notion that transformational life change is a do-it-yourself (DIY) project. You're no longer making morning affirmations in a vacuum, without anyone to model your actions after. The example of your role model renders the option of not completing your to-do lists unconscionable. Further, should you engage a personal coach to help guide your transformation, you will have a visual template for the "after" portrait of yourself.

Studying someone who has already successfully navigated the hurdles that litter your path makes success more practical and realistic. With an active role model, you do not have to be a self-starting practitioner. It is not all 100% on you. You can turn your appreciation for the way in which your role model triumphed, into a power source that propels you to do everything you can to match (and even exceed) their success.

When you identify a role model, you identify a clear target to aim for while muting the potentially intimidating prospect getting started. Your role model becomes the conduit for channeling your powerful emotions into life-transforming activity. That is why active role modeling is such a powerful strategy. You no longer have to figure out how to pursue your dreams independently; somebody has already done it, and done it well. This is why it's important to hold your role models in admiration, but not awe. Once, they were where you are. If they could do it, so can you!

I found some of my early Wall Street mentors in graduate school by following this role model strategy. After matriculating to Dartmouth, I knew I wanted to spend my summer internship in New York. Wall Street is incredibly competitive and as I progressed through my MBA studies, I noticed that, despite what I thought about my precocious networking skills, the depth, breadth, and quality of my professional relationships left a great deal to be desired. I started studying the first- and second-year associate MBAs who were succeeding on Wall Street and one common element stood out: the vast majority had access to senior level mentors by way of their post-undergraduate work experience—and in some cases even earlier. I realized that I had to find a shortcut.

During my studies at Tuck, I subscribed to *Black Enterprise* magazine. Shortly after I secured my summer internship at Morgan Stanley, the publication ran this cover story: "The 30 Most Powerful African-Americans on Wall Street." Even though I did not *personally* know any of them, I was inspired to act. So what did I do? I pulled out a pen, paper, and stamps and wrote to them. In today's world of digital communications, there is something powerful about the written word. My letter *introduced* who I was, *shared* my aspirations to be like them, and *asked* if they would meet with me and share insights about their journey to success. I followed up the letter with calls and emails, and to my surprise several agreed to meet me when I arrived in New York for the summer!

I wound up having long conversations with some of the country's most influential African-American financiers and learned invaluable lessons about my career, the capital markets, networking, and most importantly, life—lessons I continue to leverage to this day. These industry titans were some of my first Wall Street role models and mentors…and I am not sure they all even know it.

I share this story with my audiences because I understand that it can be terribly intimidating to think about reaching out to your personal role models. Many young dreamers think that they must already have a relationship with civic leaders, industry stalwarts, acclaimed artists, or preeminent scholars before they can reach out to them. Not true. Reaching out to them *is* your bridge, and doing so is not nearly as intimidating as you think. After a decade of doing just that, I can testify that many leaders want to help people on the way up. They enjoy sharing their story when they genuinely believe it will inspire someone. They are often flattered that you have identified them as heroes and role models and will often dedicate a few minutes to tell you what they know. Moreover, I think you will find a number of them will identify with your reaching out as a reminder of how they found their own role models when they were in your shoes. So introduce, share and ask. Your role models are waiting to hear from you!

Cure the "I Don't Know Them" Syndrome

It is worth restating: you do not have to know your role models personally—or ever meet them—for them to change your life.

That fact is a game changer. The primary objective of a role model is to demonstrate the steps you need to reach the same kind of transformational breakthrough that they did. It's their example and their path that guides you, not necessarily their personal advice. Don't get me wrong; it would be a privilege to sit down with President Obama in the Oval Office and pick his brain about his life and journey to the presidency. However, should that opportunity never manifest, he can still be a role model for me or you if his journey reflects the one you or I want to take. The same is true of Sonia Sotomayor. Or Steve Jobs. Or Oprah Winfrey. Or Bono. Or J.K. Rowling.

This is the cure for one of the more seductive excuses for not taking action: "I don't know anybody." Now it is no longer required that you do. Start by simply identifying a person whose journey inspires you. For example, one of my role models is the late Coretta Scott King, the wife of the civil rights leader the Rev. Dr. Martin Luther King, Jr. I wrote a tribute to Ms. King just after her passing in 2006. In it, I stated that while she was likely best known for transforming a life shattered by her husband's assassination into one devoted to honoring and advancing his legacy of human rights and equality, she was also a scholar. She was the first woman to deliver the

Class Day address at Harvard University, and a gifted musician and vocalist who received a scholarship to the prestigious New England Conservatory of Music, where she met Dr. King.

But it is not her scholarship that makes Mrs. King a role model to me. She possessed the talent to be a world-class vocalist, but she selflessly devoted her energies to the empowerment and well-being of others. She was an advocate for international peace and justice. Her musical genius gave birth to the Freedom Concerts, the primary funding mechanism to support Dr. King and the civil rights movement during his tenure at the helm of the Southern Christian Leadership Conference. Her selfless dedication is best reflected in her words: "When you are willing to make sacrifices for a great cause, you will never be alone." I never had the honor of meeting Mrs. King. But she remains a role model for me because she showed me how I could use my God-given gift to advance life-transforming movements like *Empowering Dreamers to Become Achievers.*

Now it's your turn. Can you identify someone you admire whose journey resembles the one you are preparing to embark upon? Remember, even if you do not know them, you can study their body of work, start implementing some of their best practices, and act according to the principles that define them. You do not need permission to make someone your role model. You only need to decide to take action.

One thing that escapes some people: you can have multiple role models! In fact, I would advise it. There is likely more than one person who embodies all that you want to become. Multiple role models can help you make progress in a number of developmental areas. You can never have too many inspiring people to study and incorporate into your life. In fact, the only way you can fully appreciate the diversity of your role models' talents is by studying them intensely. A broad array of role models can provide detailed examples of what it is like to walk different paths, present varied points of view on the events of your life, suggest a broad range of solutions to reach your dreams, and even challenge you to ask different questions that yield unimagined insights.

Why not find multiple role models who each personify a quality that you value? Let's walk through a practical example. If your dream is to become a neurosurgeon, you could choose a world-class neurosurgeon and model her career path (even if you do not know her personally), choose your family physician for his compassion and healing intuition, and a professor at your local university for her dedication and precision in clinical research. There's nothing but upside to having a multitude of brilliant, inspiring individuals influencing your life.

Quote

"Celebrity-worship and hero-worship should not be confused. Yet we confuse them every day, and by doing so we come dangerously close to depriving ourselves of all real models. We lose sight of the men and women who do not simply seem great because they are famous but are famous because they are great. We come closer and closer to degrading all fame into notoriety."

—*Daniel J. Boorstin*

Ten Steps To Identify Role Models

Once you agree that you need role models, the challenge is identifying them. Here's a sequential formula to help you do that:

1. *Write down what you want to achieve.* You have to distill what you want! Document an *unconstrained*, detailed virtual map of your dreams. Write out your ultimate dream career, professional achievements, and legacy. You cannot start your journey without it.

2. *Write down who you want to become in the process.* How will you transform in the process of pursuing your ultimate dream? Make it holistic, from personal matters

like getting into optimal physical condition, to academic matters like obtaining an advanced degree, to family matters like being a loving child, spouse or parent. It is critical that you remain true to yourself and are clear on what the best version of you looks like prior to seeking guidance from others.

3. *Write down what you need to learn.* Where do you need guidance? Take an honest inventory of your skills and talents. List every area where you need support from a role model.

4. *Decide what traits your role models must possess.* What expertise should your ideal role models possess? What unique elements of their personal backgrounds need to mirror yours? What character traits have they displayed when facing adversity? What should their professional, academic, and civic lives look like? This should be your wish list of general qualifications.

5. *Review your personal network.* Now, delve into your personal and extended network of colleagues, mentors, people you may have admired from afar, etc., and start making a list. Include both people you know personally and those you know indirectly. Indirect contacts can be people who do business with your school or company, people your family knows or community leaders. Include any of them who fit your parameters.

6. *Study people you do not know personally but have achieved what you aspire to achieve.* This is where prudently expanding your list is warranted. Write down the names of history's great pioneers celebrities,

scientists, politicians, activists—anyone who embodies the qualities you are looking for.

7. *Conduct exhaustive research.* Start learning everything you can about your potential role models: education, business interests, family history, hobbies, etc. Google is your default search ally, but in this phase endeavor to push well beyond that first level filter. This is especially important for lesser-known role models who have accomplished something extraordinary, yet have a body of work that is unavailable with a Google search. Additionally, even well-celebrated role models require deep diligence to discover the true nuances regarding *"how"* they succeed. This step requires you to go deeper by having substantive conversations with people to whom you have access. Also, don't be afraid to search the deep crevices of the library to extract biographical data that is not available with a mouse click.

8. *Construct your "role model dossiers."* Start compiling detailed files on each of your role models—both the ones you have access to and those you do not. Deposit everything you can, make notes, accumulate photographs, cut out articles, etc. and keep it all in a physical or digital file. At this point, you might start to question if some of your selected role models are actually a good fit based on what you've learned. That is a good thing. It means you are getting critical about who you are choosing to emulate. Eliminate those who no longer fit your criteria and keep moving forward.

9. *For people you know, reach out respectfully.* With your research complete, it is time to reach out to the people

you have access to—teachers, colleagues, friends, family and the like. Reach out via the most appropriate medium; phone, letter, email, or select social media. Of course, be courteous and respectful of their time and appreciate that immediate replies, without respectful follow-up, are far from the norm. Once you make the connection, succinctly explain what you are doing, detail how they were selected, and most importantly request a meeting, call, or an alternative channel to personally learn about their journey. Note, it is not realistic to expect every outreach to lead to an appointment or phone interview. However, you only need a handful of your selected role models to accept a meeting to start. You will find that those that do will be more than happy to help.

10. *Monitor and study the role models you do not have access to.* For this step, programming Google alerts and other social media tracking mechanisms are your best allies. Think about these unknown role models as instructors of a course focused on how they became who they became. You are their student and the only course material is observing how they've lived.

Character Is the Key

However, accomplishments, fame, and status are not the most important qualities in a role model. *Character* is. The ultimate value of your role model is that they hold themselves to an exemplary standard of excellence. They demonstrate, in real time, the kind of person you have to become in order to have the life you dream about. You might desire what your role models possess when they are "on stage," but does your character align with theirs when you examine what they did behind the scenes to get it?

For me, character is defined as: acting in a manner consistent with the values you claim in public when *nobody* is watching. Talk is cheap. It is easy to "walk the walk" and "talk the talk" when the television cameras are on, or when the eyes of authority have you in sight; true character means living up to the standard of excellence you espouse when the lights are off.

As you start to hone in and develop your short list of role models, spend some time perusing their bios, but not so much that you become enamored. The great majority of bios tend to focus exclusively on the high points of the journey and fail to disclose *how* your role model managed challenges along the journey. Instead, invest more time examining how their actions align with their words. Do they carry themselves in a consistent manner irrespective of their environment and company? Do they violate their promises? Do they take responsibility for their mistakes and errors in judgment? How do they manage adversity? Do they uphold their stated principles when the chips are down?

At the end of the day, selecting a role model is much more about understanding *how they became* who they are versus who they are. Did they take shortcuts and cut corners when no one was watching or did they commit hours of sweat equity to achieve success? Did they cover up when they were at fault or step up and accept the blame and work to correct the situation? Did they spend more time promoting themselves and chasing the spotlight or supporting others while working and perfecting their craft? Are your potential role models substance-rich and style-poor or the other way around?

Let me share a practical example of this type of character in action. As a part of my responsibilities as Director of the National Association of Securities Professionals FAST Track Program, I have been blessed to get to know Mr. Maynard Brown. In the winter of 2015, I was privileged to interview Mr. Brown, founder of the Business Entrepreneurship & Technology (BET) academy on the campus of Crenshaw High School in Los Angeles. Mr. Brown has been part of the Crenshaw faculty for more than two decades. Born in

Compton, California, he graduated from Crenshaw High and went on to earn his undergraduate degree and MBA from Cornell University.

With two Ivy League credentials to his name, he had numerous professional opportunities but he was never content with pursuing the traditional path. Instead, he trusted his heart and the calling he felt to use his credentials to be a pioneer in the business world. A quick skim of his resume reveals that he was the founder and CEO of one of the first African-American owned wholesale dairy distributors in Southern California, as well as founder of one of the first International Scholars Conferences in underdeveloped nations on the African continent.

However, when you ask Mr. Brown about his accomplishments as an entrepreneur, he does not promote the millions in revenue his company generated. Instead, he promotes the 14 people he employed and the 14 families for whom he helped put food on the table. That mindset is emblematic of a substantive man with exemplary character.

So how does a man like this find himself on the Crenshaw High faculty for more than two decades? Notice that I did not mention him pursuing his teaching credential. But because he had a longstanding commitment to being a champion for education, he volunteered to teach financial literacy at Crenshaw. As a fate would have it, the teacher of the class he volunteered at went on sabbatical and asked Mr. Brown to fill in for the semester. When it was time for the teacher to return and relieve Mr. Brown of his "temporary" position, students went to the administration and had a sit-in demanding that Crenshaw retain both the teacher returning from sabbatical and Mr. Brown.

In just one semester, Mr. Brown had made a dramatic impact on the lives of those students. Two decades later, not only is he still teaching but he has gone to build a high school entrepreneurship academy that has become a national model of how it is "Possible-Probable-Predictable" to teach teenagers to become business builders. The magnanimous way Mr. Maynard Brown has lived his life has made him a role model for generations.

As you search for role models, don't ignore people who fly under the radar. Fame doesn't presuppose worthiness as a role model. Less celebrated role models—teachers, pastors, small business owners, coaches—are more than capable of realizing transformative dreams. As I matured and garnered more experience, I gravitated beyond Wall Street and expanded my role model dossiers to include diverse individuals who had achieved what I desired in every area of my life. I dissected each role model's journey and paid close attention to patterns of behavior that revealed integrity, discipline, critical decision making skills, and morals and values. Those are types of role models I want in my corner for the long haul, and so should you.

Shots Of Wisdom

Before your resign yourself to believe that you do not have direct access to an extremely accomplished role model, think about the indirect access you may have. Does someone in your network know them, like a personal assistant, reporter, charity volunteer, etc.? Talking to people that you know and have touched accomplished individuals can often provide tremendous insights, including behind-the-scenes knowledge that your potential role model may not disclose themselves.

Make the Journey Your Own

The ideal role models affirm that the life you aspire to live can be yours. They set the resulting bar you must clear to be victorious, which serves as a guide for how you will need to prepare, practice, and perform. When you feel confident that you have found role models who meet all of your criteria, let them channel your motivating emotions which should lead you to seek those people out and emulate them.

However, don't aim simply to duplicate your role model's journey. You are not identical. You are uniquely you, and your role models are uniquely themselves. I advise you to find inspiration from their choices and follow their footprints, but make the journey distinctly your own. When I found my Wall Street mentors, I got valuable insights and keys to their success that I could use, but I did not do everything exactly like they did. I was able to marry their insights with my unique purpose to pursue a finance career that worked well for me. As my career progressed, I was thrilled to work for alternative asset management firms in a role that allowed me to help manage the corporate and public retirement assets of dedicated men and women who commit their lives to making our private sector and communities work. It is extremely meaningful work for me, just as my role models' critical work is personally meaningful to them. It's the meaning of your work that matters, not the minutiae.

If you feel inspired by your role model's courage or resolve in the face of adversity, embrace it; there is tremendous power in it. Like so many, I have drawn unending inspiration from Dr. Martin Luther King, Jr. and his relentless pursuit of his dream. I have drawn that same type of inspiration from the legendary Olympian Jesse Owens, who, in the 1936 Berlin Olympics, won four gold medals while defying the Nazi doctrine of Aryan superiority. I do not need to have a personal relationship with Dr. King or Jesse Owens to model aspects of my life after them—chiefly to never relent in the pursuit of what I believe to be right and to show grace under pressure. Neither do you!

Perhaps the greatest value of your role models is that they serve as a reminder that your consistency, faith and courage can change the world. You have a choice to make each day: sleep in late or get up early, get after it, and move closer to realizing your dreams. It is extraordinarily difficult to be sanguine and remain in cruise control when you think about Dr. King being held in a Birmingham jail cell, yet still authoring one of the most profound literary works of the twentieth century by writing in the margins of the local newspaper.

Identify and select your ideal role models and let them help you channel your emotions into action. Now, it's time to equip you with a methodology to govern your "go forward" philosophy. That is the focus of Part Two of this book.

Summary

- *Thinking about making the people who have always believed in you proud is a tremendous motivator.*

- *A role model is someone who demonstrates the steps you need to follow to enjoy the same sort of transformational breakthrough that they did.*

- *A role model has achieved what you desire or has demonstrated personal qualities that you intend to emulate.*

- *Role models are your channel for taking action on your strong emotions.*

- *With role models to study and lean on, change is no longer a do-it-yourself (DIY) project. You have able guides.*

- *Your Quintessential Motivator ensures that you finish the race.*

- *The right role models enjoy helping others and sharing their wisdom.*

- *You do not have to have a personal relationship to identify someone as a role model.*

- *It is wise to have more than one role model.*

- *Ideal role models can be identified by following a ten-step process.*

- *Character is the single most important quality in a role model.*

- *Selecting a role model is much more about understanding how they became who they are than who they are today.*

- *Be inspired by and learn from your role models' accomplishments, but do not copy everything they do. Make your journey your own.*

Questions To Ponder

- *Who is your Quintessential Motivator? Why?*

- *What is the profile of your ideal role model? Refrain from focusing on career over character.*

- *Who do you know in your network today—or who does your extended network know—that would serve as outstanding role models for you?*

- *How can you best contact those role models?*

- *Assume they are sitting across the table from you right now. What would you ask them?*

- *Who among the well-known or accomplished—people that you do not have direct access to—would make ideal role models for your dreams?*

- *What tools can you leverage to learn more about them?*

- *What does your choice of role models tell you about yourself?*

- *How can you use your role models' lives, actions, and attitudes to inspire you to get up every day and keep pushing to make change happen?*

PART TWO—THE THREE Ps

CHAPTER 4

Possible

"Keep your dreams alive. Understand to achieve anything requires faith and belief in yourself, vision, hard work, determination, and dedication. Remember all things are possible for those who believe."

—*Gail Devers*

There is a picture of me when I was in fifth or sixth grade wearing a dapper gray suit and tie, looking hopeful and innocent—light years from the man I was destined to become. As I reflect today, I realize that I was always all right; we all start our journey somewhere. But even as a young boy, light years away from my ultimate dream, I possessed something critical: an unconstrained vision for my life, which I fiercely protected without apology.

Holding and protecting that kind of belief is everything. Do not ever apologize for having dreams of significance. Some may downplay or deride your dreams; if your dreams are large enough, that is to be expected. But you must remain commander in chief of your dream realization campaign.

I have to force my audiences to think this way—to embrace their dreams without the habitual "Yes, "but", or, "if only" constraints. I shepherd them to stay on the straight and narrow and ask them to eliminate qualifiers like "I think" and "Maybe" from their vocabulary.

When I was growing up, my mother subscribed to *Ebony*. Each issue would arrive at our house and I would flip through the pages, fascinated by stories of African-Americans achieving greatness in business, the arts, science, sports and politics. Over time, the notion of what was possible for me became tangible. I began to internalize the vision of myself as a transformative leader, utilizing my God given gift of communication to make a positive impact on generations.

Each February, *Ebony* profiled the country's 30 top African-American leaders under age 30. Past honorees included educators, attorneys, authors and entrepreneurs. In my bedroom, I made up my mind that I would become one of those 30. It can be difficult to challenge someone to dream it if they have never seen dreams become reality. Yet the evidence of that *Ebony* magazine showed me that someday I could be next, because somebody had to be next. Why not me?

Each year, I added the new *Ebony* honorees to my role model dossier. I created a file and studied everything they did: where they were educated, notable career achievements, civic leadership exploits, and how their sphere of influence helped them achieve success. I did not have any idea how the magazine's honorees were selected. I also did not have any personal contacts at the magazine who I could ask. But I knew everything I needed to know. I knew that if 30 young leaders I read about every February could do things worthy of being featured, so could I. Being recognized as a one of the top leaders under 30 became *possible* because I made up my mind that it was *possible*.

In February 2007, I appeared in the magazine as one of *Ebony's* "Thirty Young Leaders Under 30." As fate would have it, on that cover was then-Senator Barack Obama and his wife Michelle. I was recognized for my investment management responsibilities at Morgan Stanley, my work with financial literacy programs at Operation HOPE and my service on the Los Angeles New West Symphony Board of Directors. It is one of the most cherished honors I have ever received. The possible had become the actual.

Shots of Wisdom

We do ourselves a disservice when we suggest that change is easy. Realizing a challenging goal is always much harder than you imagine. There are agents in the world who do not want you to change. The worst thing you can do is to believe that what you desire will fall at your feet. It will not. You will not experience transformative change or realize an extraordinary dream without unrelenting effort. Occasionally you will fail, but if you anticipate the journey to be rife with challenges, you will get back up, and eventually prevail.

The Three Ps and Dreaming Like a Child

The Three Ps—Possible, Probable and Predictable—are the three key tenets of my "empowering dreamers to become achievers" methodology. I utilize them to advance my mission and empower all who work with me. My goal is to: a) challenge you to drastically expand your vision of what is possible; b) inspire you to take steps that make your dreams more probable; and c) put in place disciplines that make a breakthrough predictable.

I have spent more than a decade refining this methodology, and I doubt there is a person on earth who has enjoyed sustained success and not followed some variation of the Three Ps. Sustained success does not happen by accident. You need a repeatable methodology that you can deploy and which gives you a high degree of confidence in a positive outcome.

Possible means telling yourself and sincerely believing that what you aspire to achieve is possible—basically, giving yourself permission to dream without constraints. Without this, we need not proceed. You will never escape the old neighborhood or live the lifestyle you crave if you do not believe that you can. Children are wonderful practitioners of this "I can be, and I can do, anything" mindset. They have no concept of limitations. How many kids have you talked to who want to be paleontologists or astronauts or their favorite superhero? It doesn't matter that most of them will lose interest in excavating dinosaur bones or flying into orbit by the time they hit puberty.

What matters most is that they believe. Kids can be their favorite entertainer one day, a doctor and a lawyer in the same evening, and an explorer the next morning. Everything is possible.

In the Introduction, I shared with you the countless hours I spent watching (and re-watching) daytime talk shows and imitating the hosts and guests. Then, an epiphany: I discovered the red button on our VCR. Now I was able to record my favorite shows and play them back as often as I desired. So I did. I became obsessed with practicing, perfecting, and performing my versions of Sally, Geraldo, Donahue and Oprah.

Today I joke that this obsession had nothing to do with the fact that I was an only child without siblings to play with after school, so talking to myself during my talk show sessions became my solo playtime. But the midst of those playtime talk show sessions, there was not a person on earth who could convince me that I was not going to become a world renowned talk show host one day. As far as I was concerned, that was part of my "possibility set."

If you want to transform your future for the better, trace back to your youth and the unbridled dream mentality of that time. Perhaps the ability to dream with reckless abandon is hard to reclaim, but you had it once, and you can regain it. Try answering this question—"What do you want to be when you grow up?"—without constraint or qualification, as a child would. No "wells", "ifs", "buts" or "can'ts". Those words are qualifiers and will compromise you before you can even get moving.

I appreciate that practical matters are important. I'm not suggesting that you divorce reality and responsibility to pursue a dream. I am simply encouraging you to remove the limiters on your imagination and embrace that "If I can dream it, I can be it" spirit without worrying about data or qualifiers. By allowing that spirit to thrive, you will also maintain the emotional momentum necessary to overcome the inevitable obstacles.

When I challenge my audiences to dream without constraint, I have to push them. Often, their personal trials and tribulations have planted a seed of doubt regarding their abilities, making them qualify their dreams.

I can empathize; this type of mindset is a protective shield that effectively immunizes you against failure. If you censor your hopes, the idea is that failure will not hurt as much. However, the trouble with that mindset is that it often shackles your ability to aim high in pursuit of your dreams in the first place. I cannot begin to tell you how many people I have counseled who were stuck at square one because they empowered naysayers and doubters, allowing those negative voices to convince them that their dreams were farfetched and that they lacked what it took to achieve.

When you hear such pessimistic rhetoric, challenge it immediately. Ask the naysayers, "Who told you that?" Odds are they do not have a reasonable answer. When I challenge my audiences in this way, I can see the twinkle in their eyes as they realize a fundamental truth: "Doubts are just defense mechanisms! The only thing limiting me is me!" The only thing limiting you...is *you*.

Pursue Your Dream Generationally

Derek Hoskin was a junior at UCLA when I met him in 2012. But his journey to UCLA was anything but straightforward. Derek grew up in St. Louis, and while he was in high school, the three people most responsible for his upbringing passed away: his grandfather, father, and grandmother. While he was reeling from this devastating series of losses, he also became a father to his newborn daughter, Christina, during the same period.

Despite this, Derek refused to allow his dream of obtaining a college degree fall by the wayside. However, that fierce resolve was tested time and time again during his first couple of years of college, and at 21 years old he wound up dropping out of Southern Illinois University. This proved to be a perfect opportunity for him to test his intestinal fortitude and his commitment to earning his college degree. Derek made up his mind to persevere and ultimately made his way to Los Angeles County, where he worked odd jobs and bounced around from community college to community college.

As fate would have it, he heard about a community college transfer program that caters to students with nontraditional academic profiles and helps them successfully matriculate to the University of California system. Derek completed that program and in June 2015 earned his degree in African American Studies and Economics from UCLA. As of this writing, he is beginning his financial career at one of the country's blue-chip banking institutions.

I was honored to deliver the commencement address at the UCLA Afrikan graduation that day, and during my speech I was quick to point out a young lady in the audience who was junior at UCLA. You guessed it: it was Christina, Derek's daughter, who will graduate from UCLA a year or so after her Father. Imagine how much different this story would have been if Derek had given up his zealous belief that his dream was possible, or had quit working extraordinarily hard in the face of adversity to make it happen. Not only would his dream of graduating from college never have come true, but his daughter would have lacked a proper foundation upon which to pursue her dreams. His resolve impacted the next generation.

Derek made the conscious decision to live his dream despite the obstacles, and he believed that his opportunity to do so was not only his birthright but also his daughter's. That sentiment is true for all of us. We all have the right to maintain a vision for our lives that's painted in bright colors and broad strokes that have a positive impact on those coming after us. If you think that is just pomp and circumstance, consider this:

Nobody is born with a guarantee of achieving greatness.

Some people, the children of privilege, might start out with significant means. But being born into privilege does not guarantee success. In the same way, growing up with limited resources does not guarantee failure. There is a multitude of people who are redefining what is possible after starting out facing huge obstacles. When I talk about this subject in my speeches, I show a slide of my *Ebony* magazine cover and say, "You guys see this? What you don't see is this," and I show my fifth grade picture. Before I was featured in Ebony, I was a kid from Ventura with a dream, just like many of the people in my audiences. As I matured, my idea of what was possible increased, not decreased, as my pathway to success became clearer.

God gifted me with faith, self-belief and positive self talk. If you don't naturally possess those qualities, you must consciously train yourself to believe in what is possible—to pursue dreams so grand they have generational impact. Implement strategies that train your mind to orient on dreams and achievement, not negativity and doubt. Here are a few:

- *Challenge your internal self-talk.* Your self-talk is that monologue that constantly runs inside your head. It is also your framework for achievement. If you continually doubt your capabilities, you are your largest impediment to fulfilling your dreams. Think of your self-talk as the voice of your self-image and self-esteem. If you view yourself as helpless or untalented, your self-talk will affirm that and pepper your thoughts like, "Am I really good enough?"

  Achievers, on the other hand, have powerful, aspirational, confident self-talk. They believe in what they can do and carry an audacity about them. The most important thing to know is that you can change your self-image and improve your self-esteem by changing your self-talk. But you have to aggressively challenge negativity. When you find yourself thinking, "I can't do that," immediately ask yourself, "Why? Why do I think that's true?" If you are unable to conjure up a credible explanation, then your internal voice is probably just reflecting your insecurity or someone else's cynicism. Do this long enough and you will force your self-talk to be more positive and empowering.

- *Change what you say about yourself out loud.* How we talk about ourselves to others is also a direct reflection of our self-image. How you articulate your view of your character or abilities is also one of the strongest ways you influence how other people see you. For example, if you are in a job interview and tell the interviewer, "I was fortunate to even get into college," you have damaged yourself in two ways. First, you have just telegraphed that you doubt your own abilities. Second, you have also told the interviewer that you lack self-confidence. If you sabotage your ability to be viewed as a high performer, you make it easy for an interviewer to label you based on the perception you've created, versus the reality of your skills and talents.

Start challenging the things you say out loud with same vigor you challenge your internal self-talk. Now perhaps you're uncomfortable with the idea of reprimanding yourself out loud, as I did when I was a child. If that's the case, try this more covert manner to corral negative or disempowering talk about yourself: wearing a rubber band as a tangible reminder (many athletes use a variation of this technique), having an affirming quote as your smart phone wallpaper, or setting up an automatic daily email that reminds you that negative thinking is unacceptable. Try different tactics until you find one that works for you. Over time, this behavior will evoke positive thoughts, and your positive thoughts will become fruitful habits.

I want to be clear that I am not promoting arrogance or discouraging self-deprecation. Confidence is a good thing; overconfidence is obnoxious. But while taking yourself down a peg with a wink-wink quip is fine, do not over-compensate in the process.

- *Stop using qualifiers.* "Well" is a code-red word. It is often a prelude to an explanation of why you failed to do something as it should have been done. Other qualifiers like "someday" and "I thought about it" are equally toxic. Qualifiers are excuses for not living up to the promise and potential of your dreams. They are "get out of jail free cards" for your ego, which is embarrassed that you have not done what you know you were capable of. But the biggest problem with qualifying language is eventually you start to *believe* it. "One of these days" stops being a poor rationale for procrastination and starts becoming a self-delusion. *One of these days, for sure, I'll start saving my money so I can take that trip around the world.* With that many qualifiers, it's unlikely that day will ever come.

Qualifiers are a protective mechanism, and the only way to eliminate them is to allow yourself to feel the discomfort that comes with failing. Stop making excuses and let yourself feel a little bit of uncomfortable regret when thinking about what you have not done. It will be okay. Remember, emotion is your prime motivator. If you feel the regret you will also find the resolve to start chasing your future without exception or pretense.

Start being aware of any qualifying language you may be using. Additionally, do not fear speaking in absolutes. There's an old saying: "Fools and heroes speak in absolutes." Accomplished individuals minimize the use of qualifiers. It is not arrogant to say, "I am going to be a successful corporate litigator" or "Next year, I am going to finish my novel and get it published." These are confident commitments that speak to your belief in your abilities.

- *Do not worry about having all the answers.* Some people are so focused on results that they actually harm their dreams because they do not have each step of their journey mapped out perfectly. So what? It may be to your advantage to not have all the answers as you begin the journey to realize your dream; you just need to start. Do not become a victim of "paralysis by analysis" by worrying about all the minutiae. More than likely, the road you travel will require you to adapt as you progress. Make a binding commitment in your heart, mind, and spirit that you are going to pursue your dream, and trust that you have what it takes to figure out the specifics as you go. You already have everything you need. Moving forward *without* having all the answers is how you prove that to yourself.

Appoint Yourself

It is essential that you train yourself to believe your dreams are possible independent of the outside world. No matter what you do, the outside world is going to define you and your dreams in whatever way it wants. We live in a world obsessed with labeling and defining people—with putting them in safe, predictable boxes. Think about how quickly society assigns *everyone* a label like high achiever, at risk, ordinary, gifted, etc. You can attempt to dismiss that kind of stereotyping, but understand that it can influence your perspective, your contacts and your opportunities especially if you are not hyper-aware of it.

As you discipline yourself to master your self-talk and break the habit of qualifying your dreams, it is equally important to appoint yourself to what you want to be and see yourself as you want others to see you. Labeling is all about other people making themselves feel secure by believing that they've figured you out: *He's just a minimum wage earning man who is never going to amount to anything.* The ugly subtext is, *I have decided that he's not going to surpass me in life, so he's not a threat to my self-esteem.* But if someone is going to label you, it should be *you*, and why not choose a label that is empowering and infinite rather than one that is limiting and finite?

I spend a lot of time talking to people after my speaking engagements or leadership workshops, and it is common to hear someone label themselves based on a single event or outcome. Students who received a C in one class believe that they are destined to be average students. I challenge them to answer this question: "Are you just average? Is that who you are? Or is that just one label from one class?" I remind them that if all the students who received Cs in Intro Biology decided that made them unfit to become doctors, there would be a lot of patients without someone to treat them.

External events only limit possibilities if you allow them to. You have unilateral control over your self-belief. Sometimes, it is really a matter of appointing yourself to what you want to be, affirming that you are capable, and then selling that vision to others. Let me share a personal example. When I was at Dartmouth, I decided I was going to be a speaker. So I appointed myself as such, affirmed it by taking action, and ultimately sold that vision to others.

Specifically, I went to the local print shop and ordered business cards that said, "Ramsey Jay, Jr., Professional Speaker/Author" with my contact information. At that time, I doubt I had delivered nearly enough talks, nor published enough content, to be deemed a professional. Most people would have considered me a novice. But I was resolute in my self-belief: I would achieve my dream of being a professional speaker. I concluded that if I believed it, other people would believe it, too.

The day, as I was exiting the print shop with my new business cards, I ran into a female acquaintance. We made the typical small talk and at some point she asked if I had a card. I said, "I have 250 of them, how many would you like?" She looked at the card and said "Oh, Ramsey, I didn't know you were a professional speaker!" I quickly replied, "And author!" She went on to share that she was a member of a networking group that was seeking a speaker for an upcoming event with young students. I think my new card was still warm from the printing press when I handed it to her, but it instantly changed the label she had attached to me. Now I was not only a MBA student but also a professional speaker.

Later, after I delivered my speech, people approached me and asked if I had a card—they wanted me to speak at their events! I said, "I had 249 and they are going fast, so come and get them." I have been blessed to have professional speaking engagements all over the U.S. and Africa since that event. While I can't say that none of that would have ever happened if had not decided I would audaciously label myself a "Professional Speaker", but I jump started my dream when I appointed myself—when I felt my ability was ready to launch and paid no mind to the world's arbitrary labels.

Give yourself permission to move forward and fully chase your dream. Put yourself out there. If you get invited to do something you have never done but have always wanted to do, take a page out of my book and say, "Yes." Opportunity does not always arrive with a warning; sometimes, it arrives when *it's* ready. Be prepared in advance to seize it.

In doing so, you will be fearful. That's normal and natural. When the fear comes, you must also believe that whatever you need to rise to the occasion is already inside you. It is extremely powerful to hear your own voice insisting that you have been appointed, that you are more than capable, and that you can be the person you have dreamed of. When you are the first to believe it without pretense, others will too.

Quote

"So thoroughly and sincerely are we compelled to live, reverencing our life, and denying the possibility of change. This is the only way, we say; but there are as many ways as there can be drawn radii from one centre. All change is a miracle to contemplate; but it is a miracle which is taking place every instant."

—*Henry David Thoreau*

"Hi, My Name Is…"

A marvelous example of this principle plays out in the speeches I do for students from underserved communities, because despite the hardships they have endured, many of them still have dreams. In coming from broken homes, abject poverty, dilapidated schools, and abuse, some of these young men and women have resigned themselves to failure. Yet I can see beneath their cynicism and their hard exteriors and find lively, sharp minds with strong aspirations for a better life.

Often, as I begin my speech, these young people are deeply skeptical. When I talk about changing their lives and realizing their dreams, they simply do not believe it to be possible; life has conditioned the self-belief right out of them. To reignite this self-belief, I ask them to introduce themselves before I begin speaking. These first-time introductions are almost always reluctant, tentative and underwhelming: "My name's Carlos and I go to Boyle Heights High School." This is a 16-year-old Hispanic teenager, present, alert and full of life, and yet he's apathetic, slouching, not making eye contact and barely audible. He can't wait to sit back down.

I can practically read his mind: *This is a waste of time. Someone like me from where I am from and the mistakes I've made is not going anywhere.*

After the introductions, I continue with my speech stressing the power of defining themselves rather than giving others the power to define them. I stress the need for them to believe in who they are and what they can be. I offer up examples of people who sat in seats like theirs, grew up in neighborhoods like theirs, possessed limited resources like theirs, yet still triumphed and realized their dreams. As I paint this picture, I can see their eyes start to light up. Slowly, they begin to understand that with the methodology I am sharing, they have the power to determine their destiny and realize their dreams.

Moreover, they also realize that all of the external forces that used to have power over them will be powerless once they make up their mind and decide how they are going to see themselves. Finally, at the conclusion of my speech, I ask them to introduce themselves again—but this time, from the perspective of who they believe they can become based on what they've learned.

The change is dramatic. That same embarrassed, slouching, barely-audible young man will stand with his shoulders back and say, "Good afternoon! My name is Carlos, and I go to Boyle Heights High School. I'm going to go to college, and I may not know what I'm going to do but I'm going to be the best at it." The audience erupts like this young man just won an Academy Award. Only this is not Hollywood, this is real life transformation happening! Now, imagine that same scene repeated dozens of times with young people in the same auditorium and you will begin to get a firm grasp on the energy and spirit of self-redefinition that is being created. It's stirring and moving. And this is not a one-off event. I have witnessed this exact scene play out time and time again.

After Carlos re-introduces himself, I'll say, "Carlos, you're the same exact person you were an hour ago, correct?" He will nod, smiling, because he completely understands. Then I'll pivot to the audience and say, "But we see Carlos differently now, don't we?" Everyone nods and whoops. "So does Carlos."

Self-talk begets inner monologue, which begets self-image which begets personal packaging which begets the way others see you. If you want to be successful, describe yourself in successful, confident terms. If you want to be powerful, think and behave powerfully. In no uncertain terms should you ever apologize for who you are, what dream you are destined to realize, and who you believe you are called to become. Never minimize what you can and will do. Your words and thoughts regarding your ability and potential are self-fulfilling prophecies. Speak positively about your life and dreams and the rest will follow.

The Power Of One Thing

Despite such dramatic outcomes, I know that my words and ideas have their limits. Some people have become so hardened or depressed after repeated hardships and setbacks that a calloused exterior has formed around their hearts and rendered them incapable of seeing how things can ever change. Their sense of what is possible is confined to what is immediately visible. Failure after failure and letdown upon letdown breed a deep pessimism that suffocates some people's faith in their ability to change anything, ever.

For those people, reintroductions and new self-definition are not enough. They are the ones who refuse to believe something good can happen until after the fact. They have an *a priori* bias that whatever they try will fail, so why even make the attempt? Why invest the time, devote the energy, make the sacrifices? Well, here's an antidote to that gloomy wave of defeatism and negativity that can envelop some of us—even you—like a dark cloud.

If you need evidence that life-changing action is worth taking, just jump in and do something that moves you forward—without worrying about the outcome.

I still do that to this day. When I receive an invitation to deliver a presentation on a topic I have never addressed publicly, I respond, "Yes, I can do that, I have done it hundreds of times." The truth is, I have delivered an address on the discipline, or done an interview with the public figure, hundreds of times out loud, by myself, in my head or in front of the mirror. Now I just have to do the same thing in public!

If changing your self-talk does not trigger transformation, just jump in and try doing One Thing. You can't change your entire future all at once, right? But you can change *one thing* about who you are or what you do—right now. Take a step in a new direction, even if it's the wrong direction. If your dream is to earn a college degree, go online and take a free SAT practice test without worrying about the score. If your dream is to be an entrepreneur, go online and commit to selling one of your products. If your dream is to become a movie director, go online and research what productions are being recorded in your area. Visit the location, observe, engage, and ask good questions.

The power of focusing on One Thing is remarkable, but not because you are guaranteed to succeed. Your power resides in your willingness to try. You are exposing yourself to a different way of thinking about your potential.

If you take an online SAT practice test and receive a low score, shrug it off. Your experience will help you better prepare for the next time. Moreover, *now you know you possess the ability to earn a good score in the future with more practice.*

Doing One Thing is all about transforming your self-image by taking specific targeted action and seeing immediate results. It is not about overhauling your entire life. Rather it is a concentrated flash of practical inspiration that lets you say: "Yes, I just did that. Maybe now I can really accomplish this." That mindset is the beginning of everything. Those words are like the loosening of pebbles before the dam to your new possibility set breaks wide open.

What is your One Thing? Think about it and give yourself an assignment to complete. If the path you are on does not excite you, aggressively research alternative paths. If the idea of going to college doesn't stimulate you, find an alternative path to your goals. Do not wallow; invest your precious time analyzing where you are going and determine how you can take a small step to get there in the shortest amount of time.

Remain oblivious to the results at this point. The primary objective is to silence your doubting inner self by affirming that taking action is good—that action can change everything.

Toothpicks

One final truth about possibilities: despite those who will try to label you, define you, and put you into a box, there will also be those who encourage and support you, including some people who did not believe in you before. Talk is cheap, but action is all-powerful. Even if things are lonely in the beginning, if you keep moving in the right direction and keep believing in yourself, you will garner supporters and in the process also convert some of the doubters. I have seen it happen again and again.

People who are on a similar journey and have a similar mindset to pursue their dreams will also come around and stick around. I call them good company. Together, you will become each other's cheerleaders, champions, inspirations and protectors. Together you are stronger. During my speaking engagements, to help illustrate the power of finding the right supporters the right way, I use an exercise I call the Toothpick Template. I will invite a member of the audience on stage, hand them a single toothpick and ask that they break it, which they do easily. Then I will hand them a few toothpicks and ask them to break that bundle. No problem.

More Toothpicks

The toothpick template exercise is a terrific reminder that you are not on your journey in solitude. Use it as a touchstone when things feel lonely or hopeless. Keep a few toothpicks in your pocket or make them into a symbolic emblem. Share them with special people, who believe in you and support you, as tangible tokens to remind them that they are key members of your dream team.

Finally, I hand them a bundle of 50 toothpicks and ask them to snap this bunch. As hard as they try, they can't do it. At this point, I thank my volunteer and make my point. These are just toothpicks! Why can't we break them? The metaphor is clear and purposeful: while a single toothpick is easy to break on its own, bind a bunch of them together they become strong—nearly unbreakable.

Alone, you represent the lone toothpick. By yourself you might be breakable; you are certainly vulnerable to doubt and fear. But when you're surrounded by and bound to friends, supporters, mentors and believers in the possible? You are unbreakable.

Change can be lonely. Taking night classes, those long training runs at sunrise—they can make you feel isolated. But trust me when I say that eventually, you will begin to see others who are on the same path as you. Those will become your best, most enriching relationships and ultimate allies in the pursuit of your dreams. They will become your everlasting toothpicks. Bind together with them and you will win the race to your dreams in the end!

Summary

- *Three Ps: Possible, Probable and Predictable are the three key tenets of my "empowering dreamers to become achievers" methodology*

- *Children dream without constraints. Learn to dream like a child again.*

- *You must possess an unconstrained, no-holds-barred vision of what is possible.*

- *Learning to believe that your dream is possible is the first P in the methodology and the first step toward making your dreams come true. Without that belief, transformational change cannot occur.*

- *What you believe you are capable of is what you are capable of.*

- *Nobody is born with a guarantee of achieving greatness.*

- *To change your belief in what is possible for you, you must eliminate negative self-talk; achievers have powerful, aspirational, confident self-talk.*

- *Quit qualifying your dreams with words like "Well" or "If" and "But". They will compromise you before you can even get moving.*

- *Every time you encounter pessimist rhetoric you need to challenge it immediately.*

- *You will positively impact those coming behind you when you pursue your dream generationally.*

- *Appoint yourself to what you want to be and see yourself as you want others to see you.*

- *If words alone are not enough to get you moving, then try focusing on One Thing: one action without worrying about the outcome and expose yourself to a new possibility set.*

- You will meet like-minded people along your journey, bind together and you will be stronger and better.

Questions To Ponder

- *What did you dream of as a child?*

- *Who talked you out of your dreams?*

- *Who gave people the power to talk you out of your dream?*

- *Were they right?*

- *What do you believe is possible for you if you have total confidence in your abilities and determination?*

- *Who do you know that started where you are and became a success?*

- *What self-talk habits do you need to break?*

- *What negative things that you say about yourself do you need to challenge?*

- *How do you think other people see you?*

- *How would you LIKE them to see you and what must you do to make that happen?*

- *What is the One Thing you could do to get yourself moving in the right direction immediately?*

- *Who do you know that could serve as your toothpicks— like-minded people on a similar journey as you?*

CHAPTER 5

Probable

"Probable impossibilities are to be preferred to improbable possibilities."

—Aristotle

Imagine for a moment that you are a 21-year-old college student with a dream to become a cardiologist. As a conventional thinker, what path do you follow to make that dream a reality? Well, you probably adhere to the traditional academic training program without exception, go to medical school, complete an internship, finish your residency, and then in your early thirties begin your "credentialed" hands-on experience in the operating room.

That is, unless you are a passionate young man I am lucky enough to know by the name of Danial Ceasar. This young man is anything but a conventional thinker. He was willing to do his homework and learn what was required to give his medical dream a chance to come to fruition. As a result, he knew that if he followed the typical route of a young medical student it would be approximately twelve years before he could spend time in the operating room practicing with an experienced cardiologist. So, despite not having any formal medical training, and while still an undergraduate at Claremont McKenna College, he took the initiative. With the help of the South Central Scholars Foundation, he identified a mentor: Dr. David Cannom at Good Samaritan hospital.

This precocious medical dreamer subsequently secured an internship that provided him with practical exposure to his dream career early in his academic studies. I had the privilege of serving as this young man's speech and interview coach in advance of the battery of interviews he had to complete as part of the medical school application process. As a matter of fact, prior to his medical school interviews, it was my honor to prepare him to deliver a speech at the South Central Scholars Foundation fundraiser gala headlined by multi-Grammy award winner John Legend. Danial received a standing ovation. I then invited Danial to introduce me at a prestigious MBA conference hosted by the Riordan Programs Alumni Association at UCLA's Anderson School. Needless to say, he was a tough act to follow!

Danial accepted an offer to Harvard Medical School, where he matriculated in fall 2015. With his admission to medical school in one hand, and a true passion for medicine on the other, combined with the early access and exposure he received by way of his internship, he is well on his way to realizing his dream. He still has years to go before completing the requisite training, but he has already lived and practiced a critical element of that dream today.

Making that happen took extraordinary hard work, sheer will and determination. Danial made up his mind by declaring, "I want to get a foot in the door here. I want a different medical school experience." Then he did research, sought counsel, and went out and made it happen. By the time he graduates from Harvard, he will have a tremendous head start. Who do you think chief surgeons, administrators and fellowship programs will give greater consideration, assuming the candidates are similar? The student who graduated number 79 in his class, or the proactive self-starter who gained practical exposure in order to jumpstart his training?

You may remember that while an undergraduate at California State University, Fresno, I "crashed" a financial industry recruiting event at Stanford. You may also recall that my effort did not result in me getting hired. As I was pursuing my dream to work on Wall Street, it became clear that top finance firms put a lot of emphasis on status. Top entry-level analysts tended to come from prestigious brand name schools (which made sense given that's where they recruited). Fresno State wasn't one of those schools.

Shots of Wisdom

You might cower at the thought of asking for something as prestigious as a cardiology internship. But making gutsy requests like that does not take preternatural confidence. It does, however, require understanding a basic tenet of human nature: people respect audacity and are like to assist those who aggressively chase their dreams. When you believe it is possible to realize your dream and are willing to work extraordinarily hard to make it probable, you may not always hear "Yes," when you seek support. However, rest assured you will hear it more often than you expect and it only takes one "yes" to move on to the next level.

Undaunted, I went on to attend a number of recruiting events at schools that I didn't attend and ultimately applied to a plethora of firms. Twenty-six rejections later, I was tired of hearing the words, "Thank you, but the position has been filled." Which raises the question of what most people do when they hear "No".

They usually give up or aim lower, both of which are dream-inhibiting acts. But when you are working hard to make something probable and you don't quit in the face of a mountain of rejections like I faced during my job search: you actually become immune to the word "No". It doesn't affect you in the least. Rather, it adds fuel to the fire of your will. I kept applying, and after a total of 55 applications, I finally heard the words, "You're hired."

Increase Your Odds Of Success

Both Danial's story and more are perfect demonstrations of how you make realizing your dream *probable*, the second of the three Ps methodology. In the previous chapter, we agreed that believing your dream is possible is the first step toward making it happen. But belief is not enough to bring any dream to fruition. It is merely a first step. Once you have said *It is possible to achieve my dream*, you have to move beyond the realm of belief into concrete action and do the work.

Making a dream probable means that while you acknowledge that realizing the dream is not guaranteed, you are committed to the kind of effort and state of mind that maximize your odds of success. You are creating your own opportunities and putting yourself in a position to succeed.

Making something probable might mean attempting to establish relationships with influential leaders who can assist you in the future. It might mean earning an advanced degree, or finding a mentor to teach you things that cannot be learned in the classroom.

As you pursue your dream, many things will be out of your control. You cannot control the health of the economy or the trend influencing your chosen industry. You cannot control personal agendas, the nuances of behind-closed-door relationships, or blind luck. But there are factors that you can control:

- How hard you work

- Your attitude

- Being in the right place at the right time with the right skill set

- Your ability to perform when the pressure is on

These are the qualities that movers and shakers remember. They are what make significant first impressions, catapults careers forward by years, and allow someone to stand out among standouts. If you want to make your dream probable, work as hard as you can to reduce the impact of everything that's out of your control. People who make their dreams probable make their success more dependent on factors that are in their control: intellect, talent, work ethic, training, leadership ability and communication skills.

There is a four-step process you can follow to maximize the odds of realizing your dream. I use it, and I teach it to audience after audience:

1. Set specific measurable goals.

2. Assign specific deadlines.

3. Work extraordinarily hard.

4. Follow a disciplined practice regimen.

Set Specific Measurable Goals

Plenty of speakers and advice books encourage goal setting, but they misunderstand what goal setting is. Writing down goals—and you should always write down your goals—is not magic. You are not writing an incantation. Simply jotting down your goals on a sheet of paper will not make them happen. Goals play the same role as the destination you enter into your GPS navigation system: they give you something to aim for.

You must underwrite your goals with measurable targets and be as specific as possible if you want to reach them. To continue the travel analogy, wandering road trips are fun if you have a ton of free time and infinite resources, but they are useless if you have finite resources and need to get to a certain destination on time. Let's say you want to relocate from your current cool weather city to one that is warmer. Would you steer your packed-to-the-windows car onto the highway with a destination of "someplace warmer west of the Rockies"? Of course not. Nor should you do the same thing as you work to transform your life.

You are not taking a meandering country drive through your life for fun, hoping you realize some goals. You are starting a new stage in your life with an absolute focus on pursuing your dream. So, as you set a precise destination like, "San Luis Obispo, California", you must do the same for yourself. This is what I mean: "Launch my southern pecan pie bakery business first quarter 2017 and between now and then, save one year of living expenses and participate in monthly farmer's markets to build my client base".

When setting goals, there is no such thing as too much detail. That is why I like an exercise I learned from John Clendenin, founder, president and CEO of Inner Circle Logistics and the Supply Chain Centers of Regional Excellence (SCCORE). A few years ago, I was in Chicago serving as a keynote speaker at the Annual *Capital Access Forum*, a conference of business leaders, entrepreneurs, private equity managers, institutional investors, and lenders working together to increase access to equity and debt capital. I left the conference enriched and was particularly enlightened by my time with John, who shared the five building blocks behind his success, which he called "*I-We-Win-Edge-Goals*":

- *I:* Invest in yourself. If you do not invest in yourself, why should anyone else?

- *We:* No one makes it to the top on their own. Who will support you in your quest?

- *Win:* Define what a win is for you. If you do not define what "win" means to you, someone else may very well define it for you.

- *Edge:* Identify your competitive edge, and surround yourself with others who complement that advantage.

- *Goals:* Set holistic goals that will encompass family life, financial objectives, personal aspirations, and spiritual development.

This practical formula takes goal setting to a new level. It also sheds light on certain aspects of goal setting that most people do not consider. For instance, the idea of a support system the "we" in the process—increases the importance of being specific with your goals. Knowing exactly where you want to go and precisely what you want to do makes it easier to articulate your dreams people whose support you will need. Imagine that you are sitting across the table from a young engineer with a terrific idea for a high-tech start-up. You are a venture capital investor and this young talent is seeking to raise a $2 million round of seed funding to launch her company. You ask, "Where do you see this company going?" She gets a blank look and responds, "Uh, I don't know, maybe a company with, like, $50 million in revenue someday that eventually gets bought by Google?" I don't know about you, but if it were me across that table, I would not be compelled to invest.

Now imagine the same scenario, but this time the young engineer confidently replies, "I have begun the patent filing process for the technology and intend to license it to Fortune 500 companies and IT executives with whom I already have relationships, ultimately creating a high-margin business with annual revenues in the $250 million range in five years, and positioned for a liquidity event in seven to ten years." Now *that* is specific. That's an entrepreneur who will get my attention…and possibly my money, too.

Another powerful component of the "I-We-Win-Edge-Goals" formula is the concept of defining what a win is for you. Many people set goals based on what they think they are supposed to want. Others base their goals on public opinion or worse, public perception. That approach is incredibly limiting to your potential. Try this challenge: make money, status, and possessions secondary for a moment and define what total success looks like for you? What would it mean for you to "win" at life? Would it mean taking care of your family so they would be financially secure for the rest of their lives? Living on the road and traveling the world without a permanent address? Working part-time and spending the rest of your time on a hobby you are passionate about, such as composing music or designing custom surfboards? What is your version of a win? It will not look like anyone else's, nor should it.

Quote

"Opportunity is missed by most people because it is dressed in overalls and looks like work."

—*Thomas Edison*

The last component of "I-We-Win-Edge-Goals" that I want to stress is that the goals are holistic. They are not just about income, title or recognition. Those things are important, but they don't make up the sum total of a person's life. Right now, you have the freedom to choose goals for every facet of your life, so do it. Even if you can't fully execute on each goal now, you must exercise your power to consider them. Now is the time to declare what you want your personal life to look like, how you want to give back to your community, and how you want to better yourself emotionally, spiritually, and intellectually. That declaration is a critical precursor to implementing a sustainable plan of execution.

There is a practical reason for simultaneously setting goals in all of these areas: you are less likely to sabotage your career and financial success when you have a plan for your *entire* life together. Think about how many people who have lost their position, status and accolades because they made decisions in their personal lives that destroyed their families, or engaged in corrupt business practices as a short cut to success? If those same people had detailed goals for their values and personal growth, they might have avoided such scandals. When family, health, morals and spirituality are firmly grounded, you can avoid making decisions or behaving in ways that might cost you everything.

A couple more important points about proper goal setting:

- *Journal your progress.* It does not matter whether you use an old fashioned journal and a pen or a blog on Tumblr or WordPress—keep a written record of the things that happen as you progress toward your dreams. I challenge my audiences to keep a journal of the people they meet, their choices and outcomes, dream ideas or jobs and so on. Your journal is a daily download of your progress, an unedited repository of your feelings as stretch yourself, making it a powerful motivational tool. Consistent journaling provides tangible evidence of how far you have come. When you feel discouraged, it is easy to become cynical, negative and forget how much you have achieved. But when you reflect on journal entry number one, and then number 200, you will see how much progress you have made.

- *Study your role model's plan.* How did your role models go about achieving their extraordinary goals? What was the blueprint? What patterns do you see? What are the consistent factors? What are the necessities, the must-dos? What qualities do all your role models possess? How can you emulate those same qualities while pursuing your own goals? Take critical inventory of those qualities and necessities as they exist in your life right now. Do you have everything it takes to follow in your role model's footsteps? If not, what do you need to do?

Assign Specific Deadlines

Being specific also applies to *when* you want to achieve your goals. There's an old saying: "A goal is a dream with a deadline." If you want to achieve something extraordinary, give yourself a detailed timeline and include milestones.

This does not mean you will succeed in achieving everything by your deadline. The point is to appreciate how a deadline affects you psychologically. Deadlines focus us, create a sense of urgency that gets adrenaline pumping, and lends structure to what we need to do by limiting the time we have to do it. Face it, if your goal is to start your own small business, a deadline of "someday" is like a blank check. But if you say, "I will open my doors to my small business 18 months from today," you are going to act faster and with greater urgency. Deadlines work.

Know what makes them work even better? Making them inevitable. More specifically, a commitment that makes it near-impossible for you to retreat: telling friends and family what you are doing, submitting your notice at work, prepaying for a trip, taking out a loan with a specified repayment date, etc. When you self-impose consequences for actions or lack of action, you are emotionally incentivized to follow through on your plans, even with a tight deadline. Self-imposed deadlines and commitments require you to be accountable to yourself. They also require you to be accountable to others who believe in you.

I am not suggesting you take draconian measures to keep you motivated. But you will need motivation from time to time. We all do. We all have moments when we fall short or are tempted to give up. Deadlines and incentives keep you on the horse when you want to dismount. So be bold and set precise deadlines for your milestone achievements: "I will be living in San Francisco and showing my art at a minimum of a dozen galleries by May 1, 2018." It does not matter how remote the goal may seem today; set it and be specific. Then you can start working extraordinarily hard to make it happen.

Work Extraordinarily Hard

When I talk about making something probable, I am talking about working *extraordinarily* hard. There is simply no substitute for it. The third President of the United States, Thomas Jefferson, said, "I am a great believer in luck, and I find the harder I work, the more I have of it." In other words, if you want to tilt the probability of good things happening in your favor, be prepared to work harder than you have ever worked before.

Even if you are blessed with tremendous natural talent, that talent must be combined with hard work if you are going to maximize your potential. Bestselling novelist Stephen King once said, "Talent is cheaper than table salt. What separates the talented individual from the successful one is a lot of hard work." Consider a pro basketball player you might have heard of, Kobe Bryant. Extraordinary talent, right? Drafted out of Pennsylvania's Lower Merion high school into the NBA at age 17, and 20 seasons later he has had a career that will rank as one of the best of all time. A great talent, to be sure. But it's easy to overlook the ferocious off-the-court work ethic that has kept Kobe a perennial All Star for two decades. His offseason workouts are legendary; it's rumored that he takes *700-1000 jump shots* every single day of the offseason. How many jump shots are you prepared to shoot every single day?

How hard are you prepared to practice your craft in order to become the best? Are you prepared to practice with tremendous intensity in solitude without an audience? Stephen King writes every day except Christmas and his birthday. In a 1993 study conducted at the Max Planck Institute for Human Development in Berlin, elite student violinists spent three-and-a-half hours practicing their instrument daily in order to get the absolute maximum out of their talent. Get the following statement ingrained in your mind—and I cannot stress this enough:

Making your dream probable will require you to work harder
than you have ever worked in your life.

Prepare yourself to work that hard as you prepare to chase your dream so the intensity of the work will not shock you. How you "frame" the work also has a great deal to do with your ability to sustain that effort. Hard work viewed as a means to an end can be a pleasure; at the very least, it should be viewed as a learning opportunity. When I obtained my first internship at a local stock brokerage firm, I started off doing what some people see as menial tasks: folding and stuffing envelopes, answering phones, and populating spreadsheets. Classic, right? Ambitious young scholar at the Fresno State's Craig School of Business starts on the ground floor in the humblest of roles. But I made it work for me by turning the repetitive work into an advantage.

There are two types of people who fold and stuff envelopes, answer phones and populate spreadsheets: people who fold and stuff, answer phones, and populate spreadsheets, and people who *read* while they fold and stuff, and who *think* about why investment clients are calling when they answer phones, and who *project* the impact of certain calculations when populating spreadsheets. I chose the latter. I read everything about the company and finance that I could get my hands on: trades, transactions, quarterly reports, you name it. I pretended to answer every question that clients called with even though I was just taking or returning messages. I calculated portfolio returns based on the data I was inputting. I turned stuffing envelopes, answering phones, and populating spreadsheets into a real-life, hands-on financial laboratory.

If you are passionate enough about your dream, you will redefine the concept of work as something grand, a great challenge, even something to revere. Make no mistake, the work does not become less grueling, but there is a deeper meaning behind it that keeps you going. From 1957-1968, it is estimated that Dr. Martin Luther King, Jr., traveled six million miles, approximately the equivalent of flying from California to New York 200 times each year. It is estimated that he spoke on equality and justice at least 2,500 times during that span—the equivalent of four out of seven days every week until he was promoted to heaven.

Are you ready to travel six million miles in pursuit of your dream? Are you ready to commit the time and repetitions to be extraordinary? If not, go back to the Possible step, because it is not possible to realize a dream if you can't do the work to make it probable.

Follow a Disciplined Practice Regimen

Now that you have your dream with a deadline and have committed yourself to working harder than you ever imagined, you need to do the work regularly, like clockwork. In whatever direction your dream takes you, you are striving for what is known as *unconscious competence*. Repetitive, disciplined work and practice will get you there.

What is unconscious competence? It is the final stage of a four-stage "conscious competence learning model" for any new skill, first discussed by psychologist Noel Burch in the 1970s. According to this model, a person learning any new skill passes through four distinct stages of aptitude:

- *Unconscious incompetence*—You don't know what you don't know. You are blinded to the reality of your own deficits and may think you are more proficient than you truly are. Novice writers who think their books should be on the *New York Times* bestseller list and fledgling house flippers who cannot figure out why they are not real estate moguls overnight are two examples. This could also be called the "making a fool of yourself" stage.

- *Conscious incompetence*—Now you are starting to realize just how little you know and how much work needs to be done to master the skill. You recognize your deficiencies and stop pretending you know what you are doing. This is typically where real learning begins.

- *Conscious competence*—You have started to develop some skill, but demonstrating it takes absolute concentration. For example, a novice golfer taking an eternity to hit a tee shot because she is mentally walking through the mechanics and reminding herself about transferring her weight, rotating through the torso and following through.

- *Unconscious competence*—Do the same thing, the same way, repeatedly, over a period of time and you can consistently perform well without thinking. The skill becomes second nature; muscle memory and instincts take over. Think of a Major League baseball player who has put thousands of hours in the batting cage and as a result makes it appear that hitting a 95 mph fastball is easy, or a saxophone player who can instantly perform an improvisational solo with an entire concert orchestra without a trace of sheet music. What appears effortless actually demands thousands of hours of practice.

Your disciplined practice requires you to have a plan and to work the plan. You put your head down, do not worry about the results, and do what you need to do every single day. You fall in love with the process of working. If you put in the work, the results will come. People will notice. Your performance will stand out. You will be presented with breakthrough opportunities.

But having a disciplined practice is about more than just putting in hours. It also requires you to consciously live like the person you want to become. Your disciplined practice will demand that you learn as much as you can about the path you are on—and where you want that path to lead—in order to become someone who can walk that path in the real world. Do what you can to simulate the end result *today*. Is there anything you can be doing right now that gives you at least a piece of your dream? If the answer is yes, do it now!

For example, let's say your dream is to attend culinary school and then open your own restaurant. That is a laudable dream, particularly given the fickle nature of the restaurant business. How can you learn about the business today while you are attending school, or working in another industry? Go get a job at a restaurant. I am not talking about waiting tables and collecting tips. I'm talking about rolling up your sleeves and asking a restaurant manager to give you a shot in the back of the kitchen. Aim to pick up a shift or two as a line cook, and learn everything you can—not just about how the kitchen runs, but about how the *business* runs. Work your way up to sous chef or restaurant manager? Why not? Why risk everything when you can get a real-world education with someone who has had success in your desired arena?

A disciplined practice should sharpen your skills while providing practical education in your chosen field. It will also give you tangible evidence that your dream is closer to fruition, and the signs of progress can make the journey more enjoyable. To be clear, this is not extracurricular activity. This is your extra job, your extra class. You're competing while you have a safety net so you can learn what it is really going to take to make your dream probable. It demands the same discipline and committed work ethic as your classes, current job, or anything else you want.

Is there something you can do *right now* that can introduce you to the world that you aspire to be part of? I'll bet there is. It could be as simple as watching a series of YouTube videos that shows you how to do what you want to do. Think about it: if you followed a disciplined daily regimen of watching videos that taught you critical skills in woodworking or writing computer code, in a matter of months you would have established a foundation upon which you could build toward unconscious competence!

There is also a degree of "fake it 'til you make it" to this. You need a certain level of audacity and just plain guts to walk into a restaurant, insist on a job and start asking questions about every aspect of the business. But audacity—believing in your dream before anyone else does—is a prerequisite as you strive for excellence. Real dreamers throw themselves into deep water and find the confidence to swim. That same audacious spirit and confidence reside in you too. Now is the time to unleash it!

Create Your Probable Dream Plan

After all four of these essentials are in place—set specific measurable goals, assign specific deadlines, work extraordinarily hard, and follow a disciplined practice regimen—it is time to create the plan that will take you from possible to probable.

Your plan is a series of steps you must take in order to realize your dream. If you are like my aspiring cardiologist friend, Danial Ceasar, that series of steps might look like this:

    a. Graduate from medical school in the top ten percent of my class.

    b. Develop personal relationships with top researchers to learn the latest cutting-edge medical procedures.

    c. Leverage those relationships to secure an internship at one of the country's top five cardiology hospitals.

d. Continue my observations of in-situ procedures and journal the lessons of my experiences.

e. Be appointed to a research team as an apprentice and coauthor an award-winning white paper published in a reputable medical journal.

f. Pursue my formal residency at Johns Hopkins.

How do you know the precise steps you need to follow, especially now, when you are just starting? You can obtain the basics from your role models, real and virtual. Use their experiences and the steps they followed as a template. Distill their experiences down to the essentials, the difference makers. What are the consistent things your role models did that prepared them for the next level? What did they do that you can do? What are the necessities—degrees, certifications, fieldwork, training—that you must have? What personal qualities do your role models embody that you can emulate? Optimism? A strict moral code? Developing those qualities is a matter of choice and follow-through.

Your Probable Dream Plan is an inventory of what you have today and the skills, talents, experiences and exposures needed to reach your dream. You can think of it as your bridge over a chasm: you are standing on one side in the present, and on the other side is your future. In the chasm are all the skills, people, and hard work required to reach your dream. Your plan is the bridge.

Here is the Probable Dream Plan Template:

RAMSEY JAY, JR. "PROBABLE" DREAM PLAN

My dream:

_____

_____

My "Gap":

Skills / experience I must have to reach my dreams:

_____

_____

_____

_____

Role models I can emulate to help me bridge my gap:

_____

_____

My disciplined practice regimen - Repetitive skill development:

_____

_____

Real world experience:

_____

_____

My milestones to achieve with specific deadlines:

_____

_____

The mental attributes / attitudes I must embody:

_____

_____

_____

Use this template to help you create your 'Probable Dream Plan' and then commit to it. Make it your personal oath document, something you live by daily. You cannot allow your plan to collect dust. One of the main reasons the 'Probable Dream Plan' is important (apart from your desire to fulfill your dreams) is that you will encounter a certain amount of gravitational pull from your old self trying to drag you back to where you are today.

Going Public

A proven method to confront the negative commentary you may receive is to be public about your plan and dreams. Post your journal on a social network or simply post regularly about what work you are doing to make your dream probable. Do not brag; be humble. Seek advice and feedback. Do this consistently and over time you will attract supporters and advisors who rightfully admire your passion and will freely share their knowledge and experience.

That is normal; expect it. Naysayers will remind you how improbable your dream is because they are insecure about their inability to realize their own dreams. You will be seduced to return to the comfort of the familiar. At some point you may become discouraged. Each of these forces exerts a certain pull on you. The accumulation of those incremental forces is the reason that some people make real progress towards change but end up losing focus and regressing. Their actions and habits may have changed, but their mindset and attitudes have not, which leaves them vulnerable to negative influences.

Your plan is the guide rope that keeps past mistakes—or certain naysayers in your life—from stifling your forward momentum. Combined with your Quintessential Motivator, your Probable Dream Plan anchors you in a reality of hard work and a progressive vision of the future that is full of *possibilities.*

You have what it takes to use these tools to bring your dreams to life. You have the chutzpah to learn what you need to know and set a timetable to make it happen. Do not overcomplicate the process! Write your plan and work your plan, day in and day out. As the legendary American radio personality Earl Nightingale said, "All you need is the plan, the road map, and the courage to press on to your destination."

Trust in the process and be resolute in your faith that results will come. You will become more skilled, wiser, and more reliant on your instincts. Your spheres of influence will broaden, and you will find yourself routinely connecting with influential people. If you have a well thought out, well articulated plan and work it tirelessly, these are not maybes. These are guarantees.

As time goes on, circumstances may suggest that you need to change your plan. Should you? That depends on if it is yielding the desired results. Early on, you should probably stay the course. But as time passes, it is prudent to review your plan once or twice annually and make relevant adjustments.

Is your plan producing results? Are you seeing an increase in opportunities? Is your sphere of influence expanding? Are the skills you are developing still critical to advancing your dream, or has the field changed to the point that you need different skills? Most important, *do you still have the same dream*? Or has time and experience shown you that you truly desire something else?

Sit down periodically and ask these important questions. Be brutally honest. Do not fear the answers, even if they suggest that you may need to make an abrupt course correction. Knowledge is an appreciating asset; you do not know where life will take you or how the lessons you learn by pursuing one path can be applied to another in the future. Ensuring you are on the right course for your dreams is always the right decision, even if you have to make a 180-degree turn along the way to get there.

Summary

- *Making a dream probable is all about increasing your odds of success by optimizing aspects of your success that you can control.*

- *Doing this takes a certain level of drive, passion and audacity.*

- *Your objective is to maximize the likelihood that breakthrough opportunities will come your way, develop relationships with influential people, and hone the necessary skills to deliver excellence when the chance arises.*

- *There are no guarantees.*

- *Making a dream probable is a matter of setting specific measurable goals and deadlines, working harder than you ever have, and following a disciplined practice regimen.*

- *According to the "I-We-Win-Edge-Goals" formula, you should identify people who will help you reach your dreams, determine what a "win" looks like for you, and set goals that apply to your entire life, not just status and material possessions.*

- *Journal your progress so you can reflect on how far you have come.*

- *Studying how your role models achieved their dreams will help you develop your plan to realize yours.*

- *You will naturally progress through unconscious incompetence, conscious incompetence, conscious competence, and finally to unconscious competence.*

- *If you unwilling to commit countless hours of work, go back and reevaluate the establishment of your dream in the possible phase.*

- *Your 'Probable Dream Plan' is your blueprint for progress. Write it and follow it without worrying about the results. Have faith that results will come in time.*

- *Your plan will also keep you anchored firmly on your path toward the future, rather than being pulled backward by negative influences.*

- *Review your 'Probable Dream Plan' at least once or twice annually to make sure you are still on track.*

Questions To Ponder

- *What is your specific dream today? What do you want to achieve, how, where and when?*

- *What does a "win" look like for you? What constitutes complete success for you, including family, wellness, and spiritual life?*

- *What did your role models do to increase their chances of success and how can you do the same?*

- *What real-world opportunities can you pursue that will provide hands-on experience in your desired field while you are still learning?*

- *What does your disciplined practice regimen look like? How often do you work on your skills? What does that work look like? Who are you learning from?*

- *What is the gap between your skill set today and the skill set needed to achieve your dream?*

- *Have you written your 'Probable Dream Plan'? If so, have you reviewed it at least once the past year and determined if any adjustments are necessary?*

- *What practices in your plan will increase your opportunities for success, enable you to develop relationships with influential people, and prepare you up to perform when called upon?*

CHAPTER 6

Predictable

"I've found that luck is quite predictable. If you want more luck, take more chances. Be more active. Show up more often."

—Brian Tracy

Branch Rickey, the innovative baseball executive who helped break the Major League Baseball color barrier when he signed Jackie Robinson to a contract with the Brooklyn Dodgers in 1947, had a saying: "Luck is the residue of design." What appears to be luck is actually the result of meticulous planning and preparation. In Chapter Five, I talked about working extraordinarily hard to make your dreams probable and developing a disciplined practice regimen and 'Probable Dream Plan'. The third element of the 3Ps methodology—Predictable—requires you to use that regimen and plan to be supremely prepared to capitalize on breakthrough opportunities *before* they present themselves.

Here's a personal example. In 2013, the Ray Charles Foundation, in partnership with the United States Post Office, was preparing to unveil the commemorative Ray Charles "Forever" postage stamp—a major honor for an iconic and beloved figure in American music history. The special ceremony, which featured a performance by Chaka Khan, remarks by Reverend Jesse Jackson, Sr., and appearances by other dignitaries, was hosted at the Los Angeles Grammy Museum on September 23— what would have been Ray Charles' 83rd birthday.

A few weeks before the stamp unveiling, Valerie Ervin, President of The Ray Charles Foundation, called and asked if I would provide the opening remarks at the evening ceremony. I was floored as I had been planning to attend as a spectator. But without hesitation I said "Yes". Of course I did! Some opportunities do not politely knock and ask if you are prepared; they break down the door and present you what you have already prepared for. Without question, this was that kind of opportunity.

However, at that time, I *had never* provided the opening remarks for an event this momentous alongside such luminaries. However, I *had been* preparing for a predictable opportunity like this since I was a child! Remember my videotaping daytime talk shows and playing all the parts day after day? My rehearsals in front of the mirror? My speaking for groups like the Asia Business Club and dozens of youth gatherings? Not to mention that three years prior I had emceed the opening of The Ray Charles Memorial Library. All of that experience had prepared me to approach something as momentous as this with calm and poise. I was ready—and it was a good thing, because I did not have time to prepare.

Shots of Wisdom

People often ask, "How did you find the courage to say 'yes' to the Ray Charles Forever Stamp engagement?" Apart from knowing that I could handle it, I also knew that I deserved the opportunity. I prepared for years behind the scenes. We rarely ask what we deserve, and, as a result, are reluctant to aggressively pursue our dream when a breakthrough opportunity presents itself. What do you deserve from your future as a result of your years of preparation behind the scenes? Answer that question, and you will also discover the self-confidence to say "Yes" when breakthrough opportunities come knocking.

The next two weeks were a whirlwind. I was managing my work responsibilities while creating something I hoped would be captivating for this live, once in a lifetime, historic event. I had to bring my A-game. I had to perform like I had delivered such remarks hundreds of times. The difference between that moment being what it was and what it could have been lay in my being prepared before the opportunity came my way. Simply said, I did not know that I was going to get that call, but I had known the day was coming and I had prepared. I had practiced, polished my skills, sharpened my delivery and cultivated a cool, controlled demeanor for years, working to make what *might* be possible, probable. Now it was predictable. The moment had arrived.

September 23 came and the night was brilliant. I wrote a rhythmic, soulful combination poem/spoken word piece that emphasized the word "forever" as my anchor for each stanza. At the end of each stanza, I crafted a line that personified a memorable element of Ray Charles' extraordinary life or character or artistry. I ended each stanza, "Forever, Ray." By the third one, the audience was finishing for me, saying, "Forever, Ray" in unison. It sent chills up my spine. My opening remarks were received with great enthusiasm and launched the ceremony with the kind of tribute that this legend of a man deserved.

It was a milestone moment for The Ray Charles Foundation and the United States Post Office. It was also a seminal moment for me: my first appearance as the featured opener on a major stage in front of an audience filled with movers and shakers from music, media, and local politics. After the ceremony, a number of leaders from the participating organizations contacted me and asked if I was interested in doing more speaking engagements for equally valuable causes, campaigns, conferences, etc. I am humbled that I have been blessed with additional breakthrough opportunities with some of these organizations; they have become some of my greatest allies and leading advocates of my speaking career.

Choosing "Right Actions"

At my speaking engagements, I display a photo of me from the podium at the Grammy Museum, making that speech with a blow-up of the Ray Charles stamp in the background. Some of the young people I speak to are unfamiliar with Ray Charles, but they, along with my adult audiences, understand the message: this was a pivotal point in my career as a speaker and I made the most of it. It is my way of illustrating that transformational breakthroughs can happen at any time, so you have to prepare to take advantage before the predictable opportunity comes knocking.

That is how you make success predictable. As you advance to the predictable phase, accept that you cannot always predict how people will feel about you, if a certain company will be hiring, or how the marketplace will feel about your product. So many of these variables are out of your control and thus are unpredictable. However, there are certain variables that you can absolutely control and make predictable including:

- Your level of preparation.

- Your attitude and poise under pressure.

- Your ability to boldly say 'yes' when opportunity knocks.

Luck favors the prepared? I argue it is the other way around: the *prepared favor luck*! In other words, people who are thoroughly prepared are best positioned to turn luck—a sudden call from The Ray Charles Foundation, for instance—into success and repeat opportunity. So luck and preparation are equal partners in the story of your success; you need both. People who claim, "I would rather be lucky than good" are missing the point. Luck will open doors for you, but you have to be able to walk through the door and execute at a world-class level if you want more doors to open. You can only do that if you have done the *behind the scenes* hard work of training, practicing, honing your talents and developing your character.

More than anything else, to make success predictable you have to forget about outcomes and focus only on doing what I call "right actions." You cannot make certain outcomes happen, but you can concentrate your attention and energies on doing things that make your desired outcomes probable and yield predictable opportunities to move forward. For example, you have a goal to lose ten pounds. Great, but you cannot snap your fingers and say, "I lost ten pounds!" and instantly have your love handles vanish. It does not work that way.

Instead, you focus on right actions: exercising, eating healthy food, cutting back on calories. If you commit to those right actions consistently, you will see positive results and predictable opportunities to get closer to realizing the goal and losing the ten pounds. You might lose ten pounds. You might only lose six pounds. You might lose 18 pounds. But no matter how much weight you lose, the experience will leave you predictably healthier and as result a number of collateral breakthroughs will also be yours: improved mental state of mind, increased self-confidence, higher energy for social activities, etc.

As you ask yourself how to move from the probable to the predictable, what right actions can you prepare to make repeatedly? What things can you do daily as part of your disciplined practice that will prepare you when luck bursts through the door? True, your right actions will not look exactly like someone else's, because you are on different paths with different dreams. However, the affirming news is that some right actions are universally beneficial. No matter what kind of journey you are on or where your destination is, they will help you be ready to perform when predictable opportunities come your way. They include:

- Polishing your written and verbal communication skills

- Learning how to dress appropriately for the environment you want to be in

- Learning how to manage your personal finances

- Identifying mentors willing to advise and guide you

- Caring for your health and fitness

- Devoting concentrated time to your spiritual walk

- Maintaining your grooming and personal appearance

- Keeping up on current events

- Building a good library to market yourself, such as a well-written resume and bio, a professional-quality personal website, and commercial business cards

- Managing your social network and online media presence

These right actions are universal. Whether you aspire to be a propulsion engineer for the next mission to Mars or a pastry chef at a Parisian bistro, you will benefit from doing these things consistently and well. But what about identifying those right actions that are germane to your dreams? This can be a bit trickier. However, this definition should help you be able to determine those right actions with a high degree of confidence:

A "right action" is any choice or consistent practice that helps you be more fully prepared to excel in any situation on the life path you have chosen.

Let's assume that your dream is to become a Major League Baseball pitcher. A lofty dream, but certain consistent right actions can absolutely increase your odds of making it predictable:

- Develop a strength, endurance and flexibility workout regimen that gets you in excellent physical condition.

- Engage a pitching coach to work with you on your delivery, follow-through, and overall mechanics.

- Study the history and science of pitching by watching film, reading books and attending instructional camps.

- Become an expert on the art of hitting and incorporate that knowledge into your mental strategy and game plan as a pitcher.

- Identify role models and mentors such as former major league pitchers or coaches and ask them to share their knowledge and experience with you.

- Regularly pitch in diverse game environments in both organized leagues and park and recreation pickup games.

To be clear, none of these right actions will guarantee that your name will be called in the draft, let alone that you'll get to "The Show." But they certainly will improve your chances. Remember, excellence always gets noticed in due time, and when people observe what kind of shape you are in, how well you know the game, and how well prepared you are they are more likely to give you a shot to demonstrate what you can do. Furthermore, when you get that shot, your level of preparation ensures that you are able to maximize your ability to perform. How others respond to your performance is unpredictable; your readiness to deliver your best should not be.

Take a moment: what right actions will best help you realize your dreams?

It Is About the Journey

All this talk about dreams and performing your best on demand is motivating, but it actually obscures the real objective of right actions: to transform you into a new person who is always ready to take a quantum leap forward. Making good choices and consistently doing the right things to prepare for success will refine your abilities, but the experience will also transform you into someone able to capitalize on the opportunities your hard work creates. More to the point:

Your journey is about transforming you into someone for whom success is inevitable.

Consider the martial arts. More specifically, the practitioner who earns his black belt. Some martial artists train consistently for ten years or more before obtaining the coveted black belt, but during that time the student will learn much more than how to deliver a reverse punch, side kick or joint lock. The student will also learn respect, discipline, patience, calmness of mind, focus, humility, and self-control. As a result of repeatedly performing the same martial arts movements for years, by the time the student earns the black belt, signifying that they are an expert fighter, they have also transformed into someone with the wisdom and restraint not to *need* to fight.

That is what I mean by being transformed by your journey and your disciplined practice. By the time you have the aptitude to deliver excellence when called upon, you also have the character, judgment and confidence to know if an opportunity is appropriate, assess if the right people are around you, and demand what you deserve. You have become someone ready to turn dreams into reality.

When I speak to young audiences, I tell them, "I cannot guarantee that if you do what I say, you will be accepted into Princeton. But I can guarantee that you will be changed by the process, and I guarantee you will end up further down the path to your dreams than you would had you not gone through this process."

That transformation is the ultimate reward of the Possible, Probable and Predictable process. You become someone you were always destined to become—capable, hard-working, perceptive, experienced, and skilled enough to create the life you can only imagine today. You are still you, of course; you still have the same background and life story. However, your spheres of influence will change, because as we change, so do our associations. Your goals might change as well. That's good. Transformational change from the inside out, at a deep personal level, is what makes change permanent and something that you can build upon.

Think hard about who you need to become to claim your dreams. How much work do you have to do to become that person? What sacrifices must you make, and what are the pros and cons of each? What qualities and characteristics must you preserve about the person you are today as you make that journey?

Quote

"Life moves on, whether we act as cowards or heroes. Life has no other discipline to impose, if we would but realize it, than to accept life unquestioningly. Everything we shut our eyes to, everything we run away from, everything we deny, denigrate or despise, serves to defeat us in the end. What seems nasty, painful, evil, can become a source of beauty, joy, and strength, if faced with an open mind. Every moment is a golden one for him who has the vision to recognize it as such."

—Henry Miller

Challenge the Plan Versus Change the Plan

So now you have a plan. You have a set of disciplined practices that will move you closer to realizing your dreams. You are keeping your head down and staying focused on taking right actions that will lead to breakthrough opportunities. You are right where you should be. But life will undoubtedly throw you a curveball or two and put hurdles in your path. When it does, it is important to not only be flexible and adjust, but to also discern when those circumstances are challenging your plan and when they dictate that you *change* your plan.

Terrific things can happen when you are forced to change your plan, as long as you are willing to accommodate the change. Several years ago, this point was driven home while I was 35,000 feet in the air on a Boeing 767-300, on my way to Turkey. The pilot's voice came over the PA system, alerting us that we were going to be 90 minutes late for our arrival in Paris – which meant I was going to miss my connecting flight to Istanbul.

Disappointed? Frustrated? Sure. Those were my immediate selfish reactions. Adding insult to injury was the fact that the next flight to Istanbul was not for another nine hours! I was lamenting the fact that I would have to spend a day at the airport and miss all of the activities planned in Istanbul for the next day. However, after I changed my ticket and settled down, I realized that while the details of my travel were out of my control, my responses and attitudes towards the change in my plans were very much *in* my control.

I realized that the nine-hour layover would give me the opportunity to spend the day in Paris, a city I had never visited. I absorbed a new culture, took in breathtaking sights in one of the world's most dynamic cities, and viewed one of the world's most breathtaking landmarks, The Arc de Triomphe with its Tomb of the Unknown Soldier at the base. The unexpected change in my travel plans yielded a life lesson much more important than how to successfully manage an international airport layover. It taught me that while planning is vital to success, some of life's great experiences are the result of our ability to manage when things do not go according to plan.

Inevitably, unexpected events will challenge your plan. Maybe a recession hits the industry you were dreaming to land a job in, or you fail to raise the seed capital for your startup venture. When circumstances change, ask yourself the following: Are these circumstances that simply challenge your plan and force you to stretch beyond your comfort zone, or do they mean that changing your plan is not only necessary but also the correct strategic move?

Your plan should always be forcing you to stretch and expand your comfort zone. That is healthy. I was forced to stretch during my long layover in Paris, but my underlying plan did not change; I was still bound for Istanbul. But there will be times when your original plan becomes obsolete. When that occurs it is crucial that you also change your assumptions about what a "win" looks like.

What if someone in your family becomes ill and you need to contribute to their care, resulting in a delay in the pursuit of your dream? What if the chance of a lifetime requires relocating to the other side of the globe? Wisdom means discerning when certain challenges render your original plan ineffective—at least, in its current form.

When that happens, do not be afraid to set it aside and write a new plan. After all, you will retain all the growth and learning you have done thus far. The countless hours of practice and refinement will still benefit you.

You'll simply harness them as you execute your new strategy while being resolute in your faith that everything else will fall into place.

Results Will Come

Let's fast-forward three years into the future. You have worked extraordinarily hard, stayed laser focused on your milestones and goals, course corrected when necessary, broadened your sphere of influence with the right people, and attended high-level networking events. What now? Is there a magic switch to flip that instantly converts all this planning into action?

First of all, what you are doing *is* action. Taking classes, learning from mentors, honing your analytical skills, networking, saving money, writing business plans—whatever you are doing as part of your practice, there is nothing passive or haphazard about any of it. But to the question: no, there is no magic switch to flip. Eventually, in due time, all roads will converge, yielding an opportunity for a major breakthrough.

> *If you consistently practice right actions and strive for excellence, predictable opportunities for a breakthrough will arise, and tremendous results will follow.*

If you make smart decisions and employ a disciplined work ethic, you will form a solid foundation upon which you can perform at the highest level. I witnessed a superb example of this at the preseason training camp of the Dallas Cowboys, one of the most successful franchises in NFL history. The Cowboys train in Oxnard, California, just up the freeway from my hometown of Ventura, and a few years ago I attended their training camp.

Bill Parcells was the team's head coach at the time, and he led a practice session that included the following four periods:

1. A team walk-through that required the players to *learn* the fundamentals.

2. Individual position drills that required each player to *repeat* their specific assignments on each play.

3. Practicing offensive, defensive, and special team's schemes at game *speed* while simulating various game scenarios.

4. Offense versus defense live scrimmaging which required the players to *execute* the previous three periods.

It was not glamorous. It was grueling, hard work. As I left practice, and reminisced about the three years I spent playing for the Ventura High School varsity football team, I realized that we had used a similar *learn, repeat, speed, execute* process to master each week's game plan. Monday was our learning day, Tuesday was our repetition day, Wednesday was our speed day, Thursday was our walk through, and Friday was our execution day, or game night. The best football players in the world were using a preparation formula that was nearly identical to the one our high school team used.

That principle still resonates deeply with me today. World-class athletes were repeating the same plays, over and over, with monotonous precision. They were practicing this way twice a day, for weeks, during preseason training camp. There was a simple magic and an authentic science in their preparation. They knew—as I knew—that process would infuse them with an extraordinary ability to perform at their best when the pressure was on. With eight Super Bowls to their credit at the time, the Cowboys had definitely prepared to perform when the predictable opportunity to make big plays arrived.

Consistently taking right actions, repeating processes that enable you to perform at an elite level, and gaining experience always pay off. Of course, while you're doing all these things, your patience to see the payoff will be tested. When you are putting in long hours day after day with few results to show for it, you can feel like you are on a hamster wheel. But you are not just going through pointless repetitive motions. Satisfaction is coming. Your breakthrough will appear when the right people take notice (many of whom have been watching you without your knowledge), engage in what you have been doing, and are so inspired by your work they cannot rationalize *not* giving you a chance.

This opportunity will come after you apply for a position and ace the interview or aptitude test. It will come after you launch your technology start-up and are clearly more prepared than the competition. It will come after others wilt under pressure and you stand firm trusting in your plan. It will come when the going gets tough and you discover that you have a superior reservoir of will, a sharper mind, a network with better resources and more practical experience than any of your peers.

You must have faith in the process. Consistent work, refinement and experience *always* lead to a reward. Sometimes, it will be the exact reward you have been hoping for. Other times, it will be a totally unexpected reward that turns you toward a different dream. But the reward is there, as long as you never give up.

There's another good reason to focus on unrelenting practice: it keeps you from being overwhelmed by the magnitude of the dream. Imagine if every Cowboys player came to practice focused on the pressure of having to win the Super Bowl. They would be paralyzed and might neglect vital daily drills in practice. So they do not focus on that; they focus on fundamentals, schemes, game plans, and being ready for the next play, game, and opponent. When you keep your eyes focused on the next step, and the one after that, you are not worrying about immediate results. You are present in the moment, which allows you to give your best. That is how you stay on task and persevere until those rewards start coming your way.

Be Ready

Here is the catch: you do not know when those rewards are coming. Chances of a lifetime rarely appear when you feel completely comfortable and prepared. They blindside you and leave you wide-eyed and gasping, wondering, "Is this for real? Did I just confirm that I could do that?" Then you gather yourself, find the confidence to say, "Yes, I can do that," and make it happen. Predictable action prepares you for unpredictable good fortune.

When I was invited to provide opening remarks at The Ray Charles Forever Stamp release, I had to deliver a world-class performance even though I only had a couple of weeks to prepare. I did it because I had been preparing for that moment my whole life, even though I did not know it. The purpose of disciplined practice and right actions is to be prepared for the unforeseeable moment when predictable opportunity knocks.

You cannot prepare yourself *after* that moment arrives; you are either ready or you are not. Either you are equipped with skills or you are not. You either execute at a moment's notice or someone else will! Ask any entrepreneur who has launched a startup while feeling apprehensive: breakthrough opportunities rarely appear when you're ready for them. If you are not prepared with skills and poise, you might fumble your chance, and who knows when it will come again? Instead break out your self-confidence and say, "I got this."

The Value of Obstacles

Sometimes the worst thing we can do is consistently succeed without a setback. Setbacks bring out the best in us: our grit, resourcefulness and creativity. Sometimes, as part of your journey, it is smart to attempt things that stretch you to the limit because of the lessons you will learn. Setbacks force you to find a new way forward and build new dreams from the wreckage from old ones. Remember, a setback is a setup for a comeback, if you get up!

Who Is Holding You Accountable?

I am asking a lot of you. It is not easy to stare down years of disciplined choices and hard work without a guaranteed reward. Not everyone can stay the course and put in the time. You may have doubts, thinking that you cannot do this, that you do not have what it takes. There are two reasons why I believe that to be untrue.

First, your dream is one that you want so badly that you will practice and train for years to make it happen. It might be to become a successful entrepreneur, obtain a Ph.D., or earn enough to move your family out of a bad neighborhood; if you want your dream badly enough, your passion will fuel you to keep pressing forward.

Second, you don't have to do this alone. You can hold yourself accountable for your results, and one of the best ways to do that is to designate "accountability partners" in your life. These are friends or colleagues whom you give permission to hold you accountable for your disciplined action and hard work. You empower them to pull you aside and tell you that you are slacking off, to ask the hard questions, and to remind you what you are working for.

They are the people who will not let you off the hook, who will show up at 5 a.m. for the morning workout you committed to, who will intervene and keep you from associating with negative influences and constantly challenge you to make the sacrifices which will position you to capitalize on *every* opportunity that crosses your path.

Recruit people you respect to hold you accountable and appoint them to do so. Do not get irritated when they do; they are honoring your request. Remember that we all struggle from time to time, and we all need someone to remind us who we are and why we are pursuing the dream. True friends and accountability partners will do that for you.

Another outstanding accountability system is something I call "creating inevitabilities". Take calculated actions that result in you having no choice but to keep going. Remember Chris McCormack, the Ironman champion? He quit his job as an accountant knowing that left him with no alternative but to focus all of his energy on training to become a professional triathlete. If he failed, he would not be able to support himself. That practical element of failure may sound daunting at first glance. But it's astonishing what you can accomplish when you cannot surrender. Do things that force you to move forward boldly without the option to look back: submit your resignation notice at work, relocate to a new city, make a nonrefundable deposit. Want motivation? Create inevitabilities that leave you no choice but to keep going, and watch what happens!

Make Winning Inevitable

As committed as your accountability partners may be, the responsibility for creating a predictable pattern of success still rests on your shoulders. If you make "winning" synonymous with becoming a person for whom success is inevitable, you cannot fail. Obstacles and setbacks turn into opportunities when you run them through the gauntlet of your mental discipline.

Dr. Patricia Turner, Dean and Vice Provost for Undergraduate Education at UCLA, has made her success inevitable with this type of mental discipline. I was honored to interview her in 2015. Her love for reading and affinity for studying fostered her strength in the fundamental disciplines of reading, writing, critical thinking, and what wound being her academic area of expertise, rhetoric. That formula enabled her to obtain a full scholarship to State University of New York (SUNY) at Oneonta, which paved the way for her to earn her Master's Degree and PhD at the University of California, Berkeley. These academic credentials are all the more special when you learn that she was the first member of her family to graduate from high school, let alone earn any advanced degrees.

Dean Turner refers to her parents as "the best" and spoke with great fondness of her mother, qualifying her as a Quintessential Motivator in her life. Her mom passed away while she was completing her Master's Degree, and while that was a challenging and devastating time, the loss became a powerful motivator for her. She had always wanted to make her mom proud of the way she would use her education to make a positive impact in society. She said, "My mother never saw me as anything other than a student."

That motivation helped her navigate hurdles during her journey, fueled her tenacity to master her coursework, and fortified her self-belief, which ultimately enabled her to translate her academic accolades into professional success. During my interview with her, she stated humbly that the trajectory of her life changed forever the moment she heard her name announced as a scholarship recipient to SUNY. That moment, and her consistent effort in achieving excellence, helped chart the path that has culminated in her overseeing approximately 30,000 students at one of the most prestigious universities in the world. She says, "The ability to play a role in making this a successful place for the students is the most satisfying thing for me."

I ask you to learn a lesson from Dean Turner's journey. She combined humility with discipline and motivation to develop the ability to overcome devastating hurdles. She mastered a repeatable process and engaged in thoughtful, consistent actions. Model your actions with this same discipline and focus, and your ultimate dream will soon be within your reach.

Find right actions and good choices that you can keep making, again and again, for years. Stick with it even when it seems frustrating. Know that with each passing day, you are changing for the better, and that will deliver the wins you desire. Remember, the predictable opportunity that changes your life could be right around the corner. It could appear today. Will you be ready?

Summary

- *Predictability is about implementing repeatable processes that prepare you to perform at your best when the pressure is on.*

- *"Right actions" are those choices or practices that help you be more fully prepared.*

- *Refrain from focusing on the end goal, because you cannot snap your fingers and instantly skip to the end without completing the requisite work. What you can do is repeatedly take right actions until results begin to appear.*

- *There are many unpredictable variables in life, but you can control your level of preparation, your poise and attitude, and how you present yourself to others.*

- *The journey is what really matters. Your actions and choices are all about changing who you are, transforming you into someone for whom success is inevitable.*

- *Circumstances may block your plan and process, but know the difference between a challenge that requires tweaks in your plan and a challenge that requires you to change the plan.*

- *There is magic in repetition. Even in the absence of immediate results, keep your head down and work your plan. Results will come in time.*

- *Focusing on the detailed steps within in the plan keeps you from becoming overwhelmed by the magnitude of the dream.*

- *Breakthrough opportunities often do not come your way when you are ready. You cannot prepare in the moment; you must have prepared in advance.*

- *To stay on course, appoint your "accountability partners," people who will keep you honest and will give you a strong talking to when needed.*

- *You should also "create inevitabilities," calculated actions which result in you having no choice but to keep going.*

- *In the end, bet on yourself—on your discipline, practice, routine and determination. You will be amazed at what happens.*

Questions To Ponder

- *How prepared are you to perform in your chosen field today?*

- *What must you do to get fully prepared?*

- *What are the "right actions" that will get you prepared?*

- *What attitudes and level of mental fortitude do you need to perform under pressure?*

- *Who do you want to be at the end of this process? Describe that person in detail.*

- *What setbacks could you encounter that would force you to tweak or abandon your dreams? What would you do next?*

- *What will your predictable practice be?*

- *What will you do every day of the week in order to train your mind, body and spirit to achieve?*

- *Who are your accountability partners?*

- *If a life-changing opportunity came along today, what would you say to the person who offered it?*

PART THREE—THE FINAL PIECES

CHAPTER 7

What's Your Story?

"The human story does not always unfold like a mathematical calculation on the principle that two and two make four. Sometimes in life they make five or minus three; and sometimes the blackboard topples down in the middle of the sum and leaves the class in disorder and the pedagogue with a black eye."

—*Winston Churchill*

You now have in your hands the building blocks of a radically reimagined life. But there is more to talk about, and it starts with Michael Jordan.

You know Jordan as the greatest player in basketball history, the six-time NBA champion, the face of Nike, and one of the most competitive athletes in history. But did you know that Michael Jordan was cut from his high school varsity team? Jordan did not make the varsity basketball team his sophomore year at Laney High School in Wilmington, North Carolina. When it came time to name the final member of the varsity team, Jordan's friend and fellow sophomore, Leroy Smith, who was 6'7" to Michael's then 5'10", was selected. Michael, heartbroken, was relegated to the JV squad, where he ended up excelling his sophomore season.

The point is that Michael Jordan was not born the greatest basketball player of all time. He converted that high school slight into the incredible motivational force that led him to become the NBA's best player. That did not happen by accident; it was the result of disciplined practice and purposeful actions: lifting weights, shooting countless jump shots to sharpen his outside game, becoming a shut-down defender, studying hours of film to exploit his opponent's weaknesses, and working on his back-to-the-basket repertoire as his jumping ability declined with age. Jordan leveraged minor setbacks as fuel during his pursuit of greatness. When he was inducted into the Pro Basketball Hall of Fame in 2009, he invited Leroy Smith to the ceremony and even thanked him for fueling his competitive fire during his speech.

Shots of Wisdom

Are there aspects of your story that you have kept secret because you fear how others will react? In the right environment it is plausible that sharing your entire story will be far more therapeutic than painful. You never know what element of your story will inspire someone, or move them, to really connect with you on an intimate level. So go ahead and give yourself permission to leverage your entire story to propel you forward and trump your fears of what others may think. Being vulnerable is a sign of strength not weakness.

You Have a Unique Story

Being left off the high school varsity squad is a significant part of Michael Jordan's story that provides incredible perspective on the man's fierce competitive drive. You have your own unique story, though you might not be fully aware of it. It is the sum total of everything you have done, the decisions you have made, the people you have touched and the milestones you have reached. Think you haven't done any of those things? I am willing to bet you are wrong, and that is the heart of this chapter.

Everyone has a story, but how we tell our own story has a great deal to with how other people see us—and how we see ourselves. Remember Carlos, the young man from Boyle Heights, who told one version of his personal story, and then after my speech delivered a version which included going to college and refusing to give up? He was the same person delivering both versions of his story, but in the second version he chose to redefine his future in a confident and optimistic manner, and it inspired the entire audience. The way you tell your story matters to others and yourself.

Often times, we do not know the private story behind the public individual. For example, did you know that when Dr. King was 12 years old, he was so heartbroken over the passing of his beloved grandmother that he jumped out of a second-floor window? Young Martin was full of guilt and shame because he had sneaked out of the house against his parent's will around the time that his grandmother suffered her fatal heart attack.

Of course, he survived the jump, but the incident reminds us that this civil rights leader was also a young boy subject to grief and moments of weakness just like any adolescent. Furthermore, did you know that Dr. King did not always aspire to become a minister? In fact, when he enrolled at Morehouse College, his dream was to become a doctor or a lawyer. But in his junior year, an eighteen-year old King (he enrolled in Morehouse at age 15 after skipping two grades in high school) decided to enter the ministry and be obedient to the call on his life, which he discerned as "an inner urge to serve humanity".

I do not know about you, but facts like that make Dr. King, and his entire story, more real, more human and much more relatable to me. That is the power of sharing the totality of your story: it transforms how people see and relate to you. Most important, it can transform how you define yourself and what you give yourself permission to become.

If you have thus far worked hard to find your motivation, engaged in right actions and done everything you can to make your dreams possible and probable while preparing for the predictable, but are still frustrated, let me ask you this. What story are you telling yourself about yourself? Are you omitting certain elements of your story because you are afraid of what others will think? Are you only introducing certain aspects of yourself to the world?

For example, if you describe yourself to others by saying something like, "I'm just a kid from the wrong side of the tracks who got lucky and hopes to make a difference," that is not very inspiring. Furthermore, it is *not* your entire story! People are attracted to visionaries, risk takers, and those who confidently defy the odds. Your story should *sell* you and the rest of the world on who you can be. What if you were to say, "I'm a kid who started on the wrong side of the tracks and suffered a few setbacks, but I rebounded and earned advanced engineering degree, and am now embarking on a dream to improve neighborhoods like mine through my startup technology venture"? How do you think those words would impact how others see you? How would they change how you perceive yourself, what you believe you are capable of, and what you will dare to try?

What Extraordinary People Do

Inspiring personal stories of people who dare the impossible give us purpose and motivate us to overcome long odds. They are what compel us to do extraordinary things. Helen Keller, Nelson Mandela, Gandhi—they changed the world because of the story they told themselves about what they were capable of. If they had doubted that they possessed the capacity to champion incredible change, they could not have achieved the extraordinary.

We all want to be extraordinary. We all want to transcend our limits and enjoy lives that inspire others and change the world. We all want to be the standout, the person from the neighborhood, school, or work who people point to and say, "There. See her? She's the one. Be like her and you will go places." But here is a little secret I bet no one has shared with you: Helen Keller, Nelson Mandela and others like them were *not* born extraordinary people. They were terrifically ordinary people with extraordinary attributes—who *did* extraordinary things—and became revered as extraordinary people.

There are people of extraordinary character, kindness, intelligence, courage and vision. They are all around us, and you might be one of them. However, having extraordinary attributes does not make someone an extraordinary person by default. It is a little bit like the old question, "When a tree falls in the forest, does it make a sound if no one is there to hear it?" Extraordinary qualities are expressed through extraordinary actions. Terrifically ordinary people become extraordinary by virtue of the incredible things they decide to do: being a crusader for fair treatment of the deaf and blind, becoming the preeminent force in the fight to end apartheid in South Africa, leading India's independence movement from the United Kingdom, and so forth. To put it simply:

Extraordinary people are those who maximize their God-given gifts, leverage their experiences, make extraordinary sacrifices, and consistently take extraordinary actions to benefit others. We are the sum total of what we do and what we give.

Greatness does not come from simply feeling like you are a great person, from saying that you are great, or even from other people's praise. Greatness is measured by how your gifts and actions empower others. Malala Yousafzai, the teenage Pakistani activist and youngest-ever Nobel Prize laureate, epitomizes this. To quote Malala, "Some people only ask others to do something. I believe that, why should I wait for someone else? Why don't I take a step and move forward?" We are what we do for others.

If you aspire to be someone extraordinary, someone who becomes the Quintessential Motivator for a young person who can influence a generation, then think about what your dream can do to lift others. How can your disciplined practice and right actions lead to you do extraordinary things that benefit others?

The majority of people in the world would probably agree that Dr. King was an extraordinary man. He led the civil rights movement that forever changed the country, so how could he not be seen as extraordinary? But what if he had kept to himself, remained a minister at an Atlanta church, and resisted taking on a leadership position in the civil rights movement? Sure, he would have made an impact serving his Atlanta congregation, but much of his great potential would have gone unfulfilled. His legacy is extraordinary because he maximized his God-given gifts, leveraged his experiences and made sacrifices to benefit others.

When you commit to taking extraordinary actions that benefit others, you also embody the four tenets of leadership I subscribe to:

1. Leadership is about going where you need to go without being asked.

2. Leadership is about delivering yourself in service, not to be served.

3. Leadership is about looking to your left and right and leveraging your peers' assets to improve someone else's life.

4. Leadership is about chasing your dream in such a way that you leave an indelible footprint by helping someone else exceed your accomplishments while still pursuing your own dreams.

Leadership is taking those extraordinary actions, doing what must be done again and again without fear and without relenting. To illustrate what I mean, let me tell you about a gentleman named Paul Rusesabagina.

You may know Mr. Rusesabagina from the movie *Hotel Rwanda*, where he was portrayed so well by actor Don Cheadle. But the true story is even more remarkable than the film. I had the chance to meet Mr. Rusesabagina when he visited Dartmouth. The college was showing the film, and he had come to discuss the events that took place. *Hotel Rwanda* recounts Mr. Rusesabagina's brave and selfless actions as he placed his life and his family's life at risk to save more than 1,200 Tutsi and Hutu citizens who otherwise faced certain death during the Rwandan massacre.

I will forever remember the humble words of wisdom Mr. Rusesabagina shared with me during our conversation that evening. Here was a quiet, simple, reserved man—not a firebrand, not a revolutionary, but a man who had simply done what he felt was right in the face of overwhelming opposition. During our conversation, he reminded me that at some point in our lives, we will all be presented an opportunity to stand up for a cause that we believe in. Despite the size of the obstacles, he said, if you use the assets at your disposal (he used the Rwandan hotel that he managed) you can prevail and change the lives of others…and the world.

Quote

"When you are inspired by some great purpose, some extraordinary project, all your thoughts break their bonds: Your mind transcends limitations, your consciousness expands in every direction, and you find yourself in a new, great, and wonderful world. Dormant forces, faculties and talents become alive, and you discover yourself to be a greater person by far than you ever dreamed yourself to be."

—Patanjali

On the surface, no one would label Mr. Rusesabagina an extraordinary man. He was a hotel manager. But being extraordinary is title, wealth and status agnostic. It only considers actions and choices. Mr. Rusesabagina became an extraordinary man because of his actions.

Extraordinary people have an extraordinary impact on the world by virtue of the decisions they make and their commitment to achieving a desired result. Many people consider Bill Gates an extraordinary leader, but I submit that it is not because he is one of the world's wealthiest people but because of the extraordinary action he took with his wealth. Specifically, he formed the Bill and Melinda Gates Foundation and took a lead role in the fight against diseases like HIV and malaria, while also revolutionizing education for the next generation. If he had chosen to just hoard his fortune he would just be another wealthy man.

John Rice, Jr. is the founder and CEO of Management Leadership for Tomorrow (MLT), a Washington, D.C.-based nonprofit organization that equips underrepresented minorities with coaching, relationships and the skills to become leaders in the corporate, nonprofit, and entrepreneurial sectors. Having obtained his undergraduate degree from Yale and an MBA from Harvard, John had a very promising corporate career working with blue chip corporations including AT&T, Walt Disney and the NBA. But it was the business plan that he wrote in the early 90's, while doing an independent study as part of his MBA curriculum, that sparked a fiery need to act that he could only temper for so long.

While an MBA student, John surveyed the makeup of his fellow classmates, noticed the dearth of minority students and decided to devise a plan to address the problem. In 2001, John launched MLT on a full time basis. Some might say that John has an academic and professional pedigree that earned him the "extraordinary" label. Quite the contrary; it is his extraordinary actions—using all of his resources to empower underrepresented future leaders—that make him "extraordinary".

At the time of this writing, MLT works with 500 new individuals per year through its core programs, and provides career-long support for its community of over 4,000 Rising Leaders. Did John know that his passion-driven independent study would become his life's work and have that kind of ripple effect? Did he know that in 2015 he would launch a new ten-year dream to create 1,000 Senior Leaders—with an expected pipeline of 10,000 Senior Leaders by 2025? Of course not. Did he have any idea that his dream would echo down the California coast and allow me to be a member of MLT's first MBA Prep cohort? Of course not. John knew none of this. But it didn't matter. He refused to be content with the ordinary.

You were born to be extraordinary. But what kind of extraordinary actions will you take to benefit others?

Writing Your Past and Future Stories

Everyone who takes extraordinary actions has a story in their mind that reminds them that they are *capable* of taking such actions. When your mission is to oppose an entire country's racial caste system, terminal diseases without a cure, white-collar crime within huge corporations and so on, you could not soldier on without an affirming story. Without a narrative running in their heads that says, "I can do this. This is my mission and I will not be denied," many people with tremendous leadership potential would instead quit and fade into obscurity.

Would Michael Jordan be regarded as the greatest basketball player of all time if, after he was cut from the high school varsity team, he had resigned himself to believe he was a mediocre player? He would have never made it to the NBA, much less become its greatest player.

We all need a story to ignite the fire in our belly and fuel us to take extraordinary action. Your story is a catalyst that sets you on a course to realize your dreams. Your story does the following:

- *It lends perspective to what has happened in your life.* Challenging times, being cheated or other setbacks become tests of character that validate your ability to rebound and keep going, if you frame your story as one of grit and resilience. Your story is the frame that lends shape and order to the events of your life. The type of frame you use determines what type of picture you see and share with others.

- *It sharpens your vision of what you want to do tomorrow.* When you see your story as a single narrative of past, present and future, you also garner a clearer vision of the next chapter. All stories follow their own internal logic; i.e., you won't go from high school graduation to becoming an astronaut on the next NASA mission. But with a holistic view of your entire story, you can clearly see what the next logical steps need to be.

- *It helps you derive enriching lessons from the events of your life.* If you have struggles or painful experiences in your past, from growing up near the poverty line to being bullied, you might be tempted to delete them from you memory and pretend they never happened. But sometimes that is not the wisest move. If we can see our past within the context of our entire life story, it can be less painful and constructive. We can analyze what happened objectively and derive vital lessons. If you were bullied when you were young, how did you persevere? What did you do to ultimately stop the bullying? What lessons can you apply in future situation when you feel you are being treated unfairly?

- *It tells other people how to think of you.* The people you come into contact with in the future—employers, recruiters, teachers, mentors, colleagues—will not know your past. They will primarily know you through your reputation, resume, and references—the three Rs. But they will also know you by the image you project, an image that will be heavily influenced by the story you tell yourself about yourself. Someone whose internal narrative is "Expectation defying intelligent woman who was born to change everything you thought you knew about millennial entrepreneurs" makes a very different impression versus someone whose narrative is, "I'm a young woman of average intelligence who is unsure of my ability to start a successful business, and I hope no one finds out how insecure I am."

- *It gives you a mission to fulfill.* Having an affirming story in your head transforms you into the lead actor in your reality story. As the lead actor, your sole mission is to make the ending of your story identical to your dream. That is powerful motivation. Without you pressing on against all obstacles, perhaps a company does not get funded or lives do not get saved! When you have a compelling story about your life and the impact you are going to make in the world, you have a mission!

What does the story you are currently telling say to you about how you view yourself? How does that story shape the way others view you? Have you considered what the new "all inclusive" version of your story should be and how you should be telling it? Have you empowered other people to define it for you? As you think through these questions keep in mind that your story has two parts:

1. Your past story, which includes everything up to this very moment, which you cannot change but can redefine.

2. Your future story, which includes everything you do from this moment forward.

The story of your past is important because it lends meaning and perspective to where and who you are now. What is your life story up to today? Your perspective on how you arrived where you are—your *personal frame*—shapes how you see yourself and influences how others see you. Your past goes a long way towards defining who you are.

Consider what you say about yourself to others. When someone asks you who you are and where you're from, what do you say? Do you project confidence and pride, or do you minimize what you have accomplished and subliminally apologize for who you are? For many people, it is more of the latter. If your life today falls short of what you expected, your story probably dwells on the negative: loss, conflict, anger and blame. We tend to beat ourselves up for not being everything we thought we would be, but that is not going to get you anywhere. Where is the hope, strength, and optimism in your story? If you look hard, I believe it is there, even in the most challenging periods.

However, as vital as the frame of your past is, the frame of your future story is more important. Your future story is within your power to shape. Your actions will craft this story and determine your future. Just as your past has defined you to this point, the actions you choose from this point forward will define who you become. Who will that be?

Your future story is basically a prediction: "I will attend the top-ranked UC Davis Veterinary graduate school and become a veterinarian specializing in internal canine medicine," or "I will move to Brooklyn, New York, enroll in acting classes at the New York Film Academy, star in a Broadway musical drama, and I will not give up for anything." You are taking the pristine vision of your future, casting it without reservation, and believing that good things will happen. You are daring yourself to make your outrageous dreams of the future come true. And why not? People regularly defy the expectations that family history, race, and socioeconomic status place on them. Why can't you? What can you imagine yourself doing from this point on that takes your story to the next level?

Is There Greatness In Your Story?

Some years ago, I was on the campus of Cornell University at the Johnson Graduate School of Management, speaking at their annual Professional Development Symposium. The symposium's Evening Session keynote speaker was Kwame Jackson, whom you may recall from his 14-episode appearance on the first season of *The Apprentice*. What you may not be as familiar with is the story behind Kwame's reality TV personality.

Kwame was born in Washington, D.C., and grew up in Charlotte, North Carolina. He is well-educated, holding a B.S. in Business Administration from the University of North Carolina at Chapel Hill and an MBA from Harvard Business School. Prior to being featured on *The Apprentice*, Kwame was a private wealth management associate at a global investment bank; prior to that, he worked as a Regional Account Manager with Proctor & Gamble. So why would such an accomplished man go on *The Apprentice*?

Kwame is a calculated risk-taker. He knew what his past story said about him, but he wanted to change his trajectory for the future. After his strong showing on television, he received great acclaim for his foresight and his ability to identify cloaked opportunities. Today he is a professional speaker and the Chairman of Legacy Holdings, a diversified portfolio company positioned to engage in real estate ventures, television production and men's fashion.

Kwame was willing to put himself on a completely different vector from his past in order to redefine himself and his future. That is what your story has the power to do. Unhappy with where you are today? Disappointed in who you have become? Change it. Reframe your past, but do not cut all ties with it. Where you have been only has the power to determine where you are going if you let it.

After studying Kwame and other accomplished individuals I have been privileged to know, I realized that they all exemplify many of the aforementioned qualities when it comes to telling their stories. In fact, it is that same storytelling spirit that helps separate those who are extraordinary from those who are merely ordinary. Which will you be? After you answer that question, let's look at some of the differences between ordinary and extraordinary people.

Extraordinary people find motivation and strength in their histories, even when those histories include abandonment, disappointment, and loss. They concentrate on how those unpleasant events made them more resilient. Ordinary people find excuses for failure in those same unfortunate events.

Extraordinary people do not apologize for the person they have become. They know that for better or for worse, their past cannot be changed, and they locate sources of pride in it. Ordinary people tell their stories and apologize for who they are, focusing their energies (and other people's energies) on their insufficiencies.

Extraordinary people are willing to put mistakes and regret behind them. They let the past go and move in a new direction, unbound by old grudges and perceived obligations. Ordinary people allow themselves to be remain bound and even defined by their past. It limits and haunts them and governs what they can and cannot do.

Extraordinary people's stories revolve around the specific actions they will take in the future. They know that they will become whatever they do. Ordinary people's stories revolve around vague plans often expressed as desires: "I hope to get my Ph.D. someday."

Extraordinary people are bold and aggressive in their stories and actions. They would rather take big steps, make loud mistakes, and ask forgiveness if they overstep. Ordinary people are timid and hesitant in their stories and actions. They spend so much time seeking permission that they sometimes miss their opportunities.

Extraordinary people concern themselves with how their actions can improve the lives of other people and the well-being of the world. Their first goal is to do what satisfies their values and makes them feel purposeful and fulfilled. Ordinary people look to procure things for themselves first: money, power, title, etc.

Brian Appel is an extraordinary man whom I admire because of the way he lives his life. Brian earned his undergraduate business degree from the University of Wisconsin and his law degree from UCLA, and has gone on to build successful law and real estate investment firms. Today he is Founder and Managing Partner of Appel & Hennick, LLP and MJL Capital Partners. But my admiration for Brian is directly related to how he leverages his professional platform to take actions that make others—especially children—feel valued and empowered. Brian is proud of his career success, but when you meet him, you will quickly discern that he is most proud of his service as the Chairman of the Jewish Big Brothers Big Sisters of Los Angeles (JBBBSLA), where he helps change the lives of hundreds of youths.

Brian founded the Dave Singer Memorial Golf Tournament benefiting Camp Bob Waldorf on the Max Straus Campus, a residential camp that fosters growth and leadership development for youth. As if that wasn't enough, Brian has made it a point to ensure that a number of deserving youths from underserved pockets of Los Angeles get the financial support they need to attend camp every summer. When you see this man talk about his love for young people, his commitment to going to the schools and inspiring kids by sharing his story, and attending Camp Bob Waldorf and watching young lives transform, his eyes well up with emotion. That is what it means to be extraordinary.

Extraordinary people know that they deserve success. Ordinary people are not sure about what they deserve Finally, extraordinary people have a clear vision of the kind of person they want to become. They may not know what success will look like, and they know they may not have control over all the variables. However, they know how they want their story to evolve. Ordinary people look mostly at achievements outside themselves— get the degree, earn a handsome salary—but have little or no clear idea of how they want to transform as people.

Remember, no one is entitled to be a great, and there is certainly no single definition of greatness. You get to choose for yourself what your story will be from this point on, and your choices will determine whether or not your future will be extraordinary.

Appoint Yourself

The act of appointing yourself is intimidating for many people. Many of us spend our lives looking to other people for permission or approval, failing to realize that no one has the power to grant us permission to be who God created us to be. You must appoint yourself to be the person you were always destined to become.

That appointment begins with the retelling of your story—the story of how you arrived where you are today and the story of your future and what you will achieve over the rest of your life. *You* give *yourself* permission to be who you want to be! No one else!

You are going to retell the story of your past and of who you are today. You are not going to change what happened or fabricate events, but you are going to reframe your past in a way that serves who you want to become. You are no longer a victim of circumstances. You are an ordinary person destined to become extraordinary, based on the decisions you make from this moment forward. Your past experiences are steppingstones tracking your steps toward the extraordinary. That perspective alone will completely change your assessment of the story of your life.

Refuse to waste time obsessing over what your story should be; look at what it is. Accept that from this point forward, it may play out in a way that you cannot anticipate. That is totally fine. Embrace the uncertainty. I did not fully comprehend what was going to happen when I self-appointed myself to become a speaker. But I gave myself permission to become a speaker when it became clear that was part of my new definition of who Ramsey Jay, Jr. was destined to become. You must define who you will become and let that new version of you determine what your extraordinary actions will be. The rest will take care of itself!

Write Your Story

So, what will your story be going forward? This is your chance to erase pessimism and replace it with vivid possible, probable, and predictable images of your dreams for tomorrow. Remember, we define ourselves by who we are today, but that definition must include a distinct description of who we are going to become. The version of your future story that you tell yourself will shape how you view yourself. If you say, "I don't have a clue where I want to be or who I want to become in five years," you are likely to internalize that and make that uncertainty your reality.

On the other hand, if your inner voice confidently declares, "In five years, I will be studying voice at the American Conservatory of Paris," you are going to do whatever you can to make that story come true. It is your self-definition. So, what are you going to write?

Seriously, write your story. Divide it into two parts: past and future. It is important to see your future story in *your own* writing to make it real and simulate how others will receive it. The following guidelines will help you author it in a manner that will help make it the transformational document it is intended to be:

- *Reject blanket statements and judgments.* Writing something like, "I'm Nancy, I grew up in south side

Chicago and my family was poor" does not tell anyone anything, but it does place an arbitrary label on you. What was your childhood like? Why was money tight? Was there a good reason? What did your family do to make ends meet? What did you do for fun even though things were tough? Each detail adds more depth to the picture and story of who you are. That depth is important to define who you truly are.

- *Appreciate the lessons in your past.* What did you learn by dealing with family trials, troubles in schools, or personal failures? How did you become wiser, more tolerant, or more street-savvy? No matter what your struggle was, you survived! By definition, as a result of those past experiences, you are smarter and more resilient than you were back then. What lessons helped you stay the course and how do they define who you are today and who you are going to be tomorrow?

- *Ask people close to you for their opinion.* Sometimes, the best way to get perspective is to ask someone. Talk to people who know you well but who are distant enough to be objective: grandparents, aunts and uncles, teachers, longtime friends. Ask them what makes you different, what makes you special. Ask them about your strengths and weaknesses. Ask them what your innate talents are. Trust me, they will be honest…sometimes a little too honest!

- *Think like you are writing the trailer to a movie.* A story can be told in a thousand different ways. Your job is to make the story of your past inspiring and exciting to *you*. How can you frame the events of your life and the person you have become to make them the plot line of a movie that people must see? Think about how the *Hunger Games* movies could have been marketed: "A girl who knows how to shoot a bow and arrow fights against bad guys." Boring. But "A young female warrior becomes the face of a revolution against a tyrannical government"? Which would you prefer to watch? How can you shape the details of your story to make it worth watching and supporting?

- *Write what you aspire to be and be specific.* For your future story, why not be as specific as possible? No one is going to hold you to the details. Let's say you write the following, "In five years I will graduate from MIT with a degree in computer science and get a job as a software engineer with Google." Will you be the least bit embarrassed if you graduate from MIT and wind up as an early employee at a Silicon Beach startup? I doubt it! Remember, your future is about the person who you are becoming, not the details of your career or social status. However, those details give you a dream to aim for and a goal to direct your energies toward. So dream big and get detailed about it.

- *Write about the impact you will have on the world.* Extraordinary people are committed to making other people's lives and the world better, right? That means you cannot stop at your personal, career, or life goals when you write your story. You have to go a step farther and chronicle how you will do your part to transform the world. "I will attend medical school and become a genetic researcher" is an incomplete story. "I will attend medical school, become a genetic researcher, and find a cure for the Huntington's disease that runs in my family" is a story worth telling!

This is your moment, right now, to define who you are to yourself and to everyone you meet from this day forward. No one has the authority to determine this but you. Remember how I printed business cards with the title Professional Speaker because I decided to self-appoint? That was me, writing the next part of my story, and it started to manifest the same day. You can do the same thing. You *must* do the same thing. Start now:

The story of my past through today:

_____

_____

_____

The person I will become starting tomorrow:

_____

_____

_____

The impact I will have on others and in the world:

_____

_____

_____

Summary

- *Your story is a motivating force for creating the future of your dreams.*

- *Your story is a framing tool that lends perspective to the events of your past. It also influences how other people see you.*

- *Before your story can influence others you must possess a sense of the depth of your story.*

- *Our stories give us a sense of mission and purpose, and propel us to do extraordinary things while writing the ending we always envisioned.*

- *Extraordinary people are those who maximize their God-given gifts, leverage their experiences, make extraordinary sacrifices, and consistently take actions to benefit others.*

- *We are what we do and what we give. Being extraordinary is position, title and status agnostic.*

- *Your story has two parts: everything you have experienced up until now, and everything you will do and experience from this moment forward.*

- *The story of your past has strength, endurance, wisdom and overcoming failure written all over it.*

- *The story of your future must first be about how you can impact others. Detailing your personal benefits is secondary.*

- *Writing your story is a practical method of appointing yourself to the future you desire while simultaneously defining who you are for the world.*

- *You are the only person with the authority to grant yourself permission to be who you were born to be.*

Questions To Ponder

- *What are the great lessons and achievements from your past?*

- *What did you survive? How did you overcome? How did you grow?*

- *Who was your nemesis and how did you triumph?*

- *What key decisions propelled you to where you are today?*

- *What part of your story do you keep secret and hidden from others? What is the worst thing that could happen if you shared portions of it selectively?*

- *Where are you today? How would you define this point in your story? Poised to jump into something better? Recovering from struggle? Unsure of what to do next? Seeking wisdom and guidance?*

  How do you want other people to perceive you? How do you not want them to perceive you?

- *From this point on, what are the details of your story? What are your plans for school, career, achievement, or personal development? Get detailed.*

- *What kind of impact will you make in the world?*

- *What are the characteristics of the person you aspire to become, irrespective of how your career plans unfold?*

- *Who do you want your story to inspire?*

- *How would you present your story like a movie trailer that would leave audiences with great anticipation?*

- *What is your 100% new definition of you?*

CHAPTER 8

If You're Not Hearing "No", You're Aiming Too Low

"Our firmest convictions are apt to be the most suspect, they mark our limitations and our bounds. Life is a pretty thing unless it is moved by the indomitable urge to extend its boundaries."

— *Jose Ortega y Gasset*

I stumbled across a video of a Philadelphia area high school basketball game and one player absolutely commanded my attention. His name was Kevin Grow and he was fired up—talking to everybody, motivating his teammates, and completely focused on every play, every shot. Kevin was not the best player on the floor but he had a great night, sinking multiple three-point shots on the way to helping his team win. In the subsequent interviews that Kevin gave after that memorable night, his comments were as inspiring as any superstar athlete's.

Kevin has Down syndrome, a chromosomal genetic disorder which results in intellectual disabilities. You might think that fact would limit him, but it did not matter to him in the least. He was the most charismatic player on the floor, and his passion inspired his teammates, which in turn elevated the team's play. If this young man, with his disability, could play well and take such joy in doing so, how could any of his teammates take a play off or get down after they blew a defensive assignment or failed to grab an offensive rebound?

I have never forgotten about Kevin, because he epitomizes the essence of breaking boundaries and defying expectations. In Chapter Seven, we talked about writing your story, and some people will not be expecting you to take your story in a fresh new direction. They will expect you to continue on the same path. If you have been a C student, they will assume that you will always be a C student. If you have been a middle manager, they will always define you as a middle manager. When you attempt to exceed their expectations, they may become irritated, even offended.

When you stretch and chase your dreams, you will encounter resistance. This is natural and normal. We become uncomfortable when someone around us violates "the way things are done." You will hear "no" from the wrong people. What matters is that, like Kevin, you ignore the contrarians. The only voice that matters is yours.

However, people telling you what you cannot do are important for one reason: they are a leading indicator that you are on the right track. Bold moves and aggressive ideas make people uncomfortable, but they are also what produce seismic shifts and meaningful impact on the world. The more the path you have chosen makes others resist or discourage you, the more you can be sure you are doing something right. In other words:

If you're not hearing "No," you're aiming too low.

Proponents or Detractors?

Daring choices that challenge conventional thinking. Innovative ideas that make traditionalists nervous. Those endeavors produce greatness. A willingness to fly in the face of accepted wisdom has helped contribute to numerous advances in technology, science, politics, and art. It gave us the radical pointillism of painter Georges Seurat, which resulted in his revolutionary paintings being banned from Paris salons. It helped cement The Civil Rights Act of 1964, which outlawed discrimination based on race, color, religion and sex—much to the anger of many southerners. It spurred

NASA's race to land a man on the moon, which led directly to the space shuttle and Mars rover programs.

Every advance or bold step faces intense opposition from primitive minds resistant to change, or people who feel insecure about their limitations. Start treating such opposition as a hopeful sign. You are shaking things up and forcing people to think in new ways, and that means you are gaining traction. If you are proceeding without any opposition or objection, then perhaps you are not aiming high enough!

Quote

"You have set yourselves a difficult task, but you will succeed if you persevere; and you will find a joy in overcoming obstacles."

—Helen Keller

People will resist your edgy, creative thinking. When you announce your political candidacy on a tax reform platform, they will warn you that you will never raise the necessary campaign contributions. So as you are implementing your Possible-Probable-Predictable strategy, it is also time to take an acute look at the people in your circle. There are two types: *proponents* and *detractors*.

If you are what you do, you are also the company you keep. The people who comprise your inner circle of peers, colleagues and friends will represent who you believe you are; they reflect how you see yourself and what you feel you deserve. Proponents do not view you as a threat; they only want the best for you. Your accomplishments do not diminish them. They are empowering, independent, confident and uplifting. They make you feel better about yourself and are your greatest champions. Rather than being intimidated by your good fortune, they celebrate it. They make you feel like you can conquer the world.

Who wouldn't want more of such people in their life? They never give up on you and have the potential to become Quintessential Motivators down the line. They are hard to find and if you already have such people in your life, hold onto them. If you do not, make it a point to identify them. Usually, they have achieved some level of success themselves. Oftentimes, they are grounded individuals who are strong in their faith, values, and sense of self. They are secure in their standing and, therefore, can afford to be generous with their support. And they rarely, if ever, ask for anything in return.

Shots of Wisdom

Ever wonder why certain people disappear from your life right when you meet an important milestone? Odds are, those people were bothered by how your success made them feel about themselves. Today it couldn't be easier to congratulate someone if you really want to: phone, text, social media and email make it extremely convenient. If certain people become more distant as you move closer to realizing your dream, it's likely they are choosing to become detractors. Initially it might hurt, but do not chase them. Stay focused and move forward.

Detractors, on the other hand, turn on you when the pursuit of your dream carries you to heights they themselves have failed to reach. They are codependent, self-hating and have a vocabulary filled with discouraging language: "Are you sure you want to do that?" "I don't think that will work." "I don't think you can make it." These people have struggled to achieve their dreams, and the idea of you rising above them to reach yours makes them question the person they see in the mirror.

If you stuck to your personal budget and paid off all of your credit card debt while they still owe $20,000, they may urge you to buy a new 60-inch LCD television. If you studied at night and earned that professional certification which results in a promotion, they might begin to whisper about the company's long-term viability. Detractors contribute nothing to your success. They are your "bucket of crabs." That is what detractors do: implore you to come back down and stay where you are so their misery has company!

It is easy to understand why you want to keep proponents close at hand. But why on earth do we—and we all do it—keep a few detractors around as well? Sometimes, they are longtime friends who provide some auxiliary benefit we do not want to be without. Sometimes, they are family, and we fear the consequences of distancing ourselves. Sometimes, we are just lazy or blind to who they really are. But while people opposing you is an indicator that you are on the right track, giving those people dominion over your thought process and emotions is an absolute non-starter.

Who Will You Allow Into Your Life?

It all comes down to who you allow to be part of your life and your inner circle—whose voice you will choose to listen to. If you are going to challenge conventional wisdom and defy the herd, you need people around you who believe in you, encourage you and provide unbiased advice. There will also be times when you think you made the wrong decision, and that is when you rely on your proponents. Detractors care about you making them feel comfortable about themselves. Proponents care about you being your best.

This is not about populating your world with "yes men" and "yes women" who tell you what you want to hear. The prototypical proponents in your inner circle do not sell out; they buy into your dreams and plans and support them. Furthermore, they will:

- Tell you what you need to hear, not what you want to hear.

- Offer objective advice when you ask for it.

- Listen without passing judgment when you need to talk.

- Play devil's advocate to help develop your critical thinking skills.

- Hold you accountable for your decisions.

That is mature, real-world support from people whose only agenda is that you live the life of your dreams. Those are the kinds of people who you need in your life. If you want to give your dreams the best opportunities to be realized, surround yourself with people who fill you up. Lean on them and learn from them. Open yourself and share yourself with them.

A few years ago, I was at St. John's University in Queens, New York, presenting workshops on leadership, resume writing, interviewing, and diversity awareness for the Monster.com Leadership Program. I was one of thirteen workshop trainers from around the nation invited to present to hundreds of student leaders. However, before I could present to the students I had to pass the certification program. I practiced long and hard and I was a little wary about sharing the unique presentation techniques I had developed.

But as the other trainers began to share, I opened up and reciprocated, and I shared the techniques I had developed with them. As a result, I learned from the other trainers and became a better trainer myself. Together we succeeded in challenging and inspiring future leaders while giving them great hope for their futures. Keep your friends close and your proponents closer.

As you prepare to embark on the journey of a lifetime, it is time to start asking some hard questions about the people in your inner circle:

- Does this person fill me up or drain me?

- What does being around this person say about me to others?

- Does this person enhance who I am becoming?

- If necessary, can I reorient this person to become a source of strength and support?

- If necessary, can I minimize the person's effect on my life without distancing myself completely, or do I have to eliminate all ties completely and deal with the consequences?

The last question is the toughest, no doubt about it. This is about your future; you must become discerning about who you allow into your life and who you purge from it. In order to live the life you want, you may have to distance yourself from people who have been in it for a while. Enforcing this principle means you value yourself highly enough—and value the promise of your future enough—to expect more from the people around you.

In distancing yourself from detractors, know this: it is not your responsibility to save them. There are some people you cannot save, and you can actually harm them by lowering your sights or dumbing down your dreams to make them feel better. It is not your job to throw shade on your light and vision. You can bring more good into your detractors lives by becoming the best person you can be.

Attracting Proponents

Of course, removing the detractors from your life is only half of the task. You also need to surround yourself with proponents. But how do you go about identifying them?

The primary strategy for attracting proponents is fulfilling your role, which is to become someone who attracts those who will be excited and challenged by what you are doing. You do that by excelling at everything you do and by being positive and supportive of others without being asked. Remember, the people who will root for you and help you succeed are usually successful themselves—confident, sure of themselves and happy with where they are. Those people are attracted to others who share those same qualities. Like attracts like.

Here are some suggestions for attracting more quality, positive individuals into your sphere of influence:

- *Get involved in your desired field.* Generic networking events are mostly full of people who want to circulate business cards and look for opportunities. Be careful about wasting too much time at these kinds of events. Instead, be much more strategic, and participate in events with detailed and actionable agendas related to the field you intend to be involved in. If your dream is to be a teacher, network with a school reform organization in your area or run for the school board. If your dream is to work in the financial industry, sit on round tables discussing financial trends that impact your community. Events where real people do real things are where you can make an impression that counts.

- *Offer before you ask.* In every situation, always be seeking opportunities to contribute. How can you help someone, solve a problem, find information, or make an introduction? Many people attempt to advance their dreams by asking what others can do for them. Entering with your hand out does not inspire anybody. Those who inspire and stand out are sources of ideas, assistance and solutions, especially if they show wisdom beyond their years. Always be asking yourself, "What can I do to make myself indispensable to this group, organization, or cause?"

- *Banish cynicism.* There is a lot of eye rolling, seen-it-all-before attitude and cynicism in the world today. But there is no place for it here. You have not seen it all. And while it is essential to ask smart questions of the people you meet, it is just as important to be honest, enthusiastic, and to listen more than you speak.

- *Volunteer.* Have you noticed that some of the most influential leaders in your community serve on multiple boards for nonprofits, hospitals, scholarship organizations, government advocacy and arts groups? It's not just because they care about those causes. It is because there is a double bottom line. On one hand, they genuinely care. On the other, volunteering is also a way to familiarize yourself with like-minded movers and shakers while learning about their abilities and attitudes.

If you want to get noticed among them, give of your time and energy. Volunteer for a board or two. Mentor young people who are following in your footsteps. Work with organizations teaching literacy in after school programs or training single mothers on how to invest and manage money. There are undoubtedly numerous opportunities in your area.

- *Be clear about what you're looking for.* There is nothing wrong with letting people know that you are committed to expanding your network of influential, high-character individuals. Be honest; leaders know you are at events and on boards to give back and to meet other likeminded individuals. Many of them are doing the same! So be direct. Share your dreams and aspirations. Invite people to share your information and your story with others they think might be interested in supporting you.

- *Be proactive and create opportunities.* Do not wait around for an invitation to get involved. Create your own. People respect proactive individuals who make things happen and are unafraid to put themselves and their dreams out there. If your actions demonstrate you are that kind of person, you will garner supporters. Additionally, it will expedite the process of developing influential relationships.

- *Have a professional online presence.* These days, after you make a favorable impression, your new contacts will usually do one of these things: check your social media accounts (Twitter, Instagram, Facebook, etc.), visit your LinkedIn profile to find mutual connections, and visit your website. Make sure all of the above, as well as your other online records, are clean and professional.

Most important, *get yourself out there.* You will not meet the right people sitting behind a computer or staring at a mobile device screen. Once you identify the right events, symposiums, and round tables, review the relevant agendas and go. Attend as many trade shows and conferences as possible. Become vested in the mission at fundraisers, entrepreneurship forums and speed coding events. Whatever you can do to get into the mix early and often, do it. The more people you meet, the more chances you will have to demonstrate that you are someone worth knowing. Then you can become more selective and focus on mining your developing network.

Also, *become someone worth knowing.* Be the best *version* of your authentic self. Release your doubts and mistrust, and set aside your fear. Affirm that you are a problem solver, not a problem finder. Positive, empowering people want to be around others who share those same qualities. So if you feel you have spent too much time cloaked in disappointment, confusion or discouragement, now is the time to shed them in favor of positivity, generosity and confidence. Get out there and get involved. You will make mistakes, and that is okay. As long as you are sincere and honest about who you are, and that you're committed to doing everything in your power to achieve dreams that ultimately empower others, people will be very forgiving and understanding.

Add Value, Give More

Successful men and women are used to people approaching them with their hands out; everybody wants something. Stand out by asking how you can serve. Donate to their favorite cause. Solve a problem. Make an introduction. Find a copy of a rare book that they covet. Create value for the person you are developing a relationship with and ask for nothing in return. You will make a tremendous impression and consistently doing so will keep you on their radar.

Who To Let In

While people you are networking with assess you, you should also assess them. It is important to monitor who you let into your life at all times. First of all, look for people with whom you have natural chemistry. People with whom you communicate easily, share similar values, or have common interests or hobbies. Beyond that, it is wise to look for people who will challenge you but who are fundamentally positive and encouraging. You want to surround yourself with people who are credible and will keep you honest as they make you feel that you can accomplish your dreams.

Identify individuals who have experience in the field that you are interested in, but do not make that a deal breaker. You never know where your path will take you, and it is more important to have a network of good human beings than it is to know someone who can just get you a job. The most successful people I know have a personal network with both depth and breadth. They know doctors, lawyers and CEOs, but they also spend time with teachers and philanthropists, writers and artists. They prefer to be around those who enrich them with their spirit, invigorate them with insightful conversation, and fill their calendars with causes and events that affect change. Cultivate the same diversity in your network.

Most important, look for people of good character, people who keep their word and are ethical, just and decent. Resist the temptation to sit at the feet of someone just because he or she is famous or has an impressive title. Know the character of the person you are dealing with when they are not in the spotlight. People of character and values will deal with you fairly, pass on opportunities, and celebrate when good fortune comes your way. You can count on them to do the right thing.

Once you have established your network, how best to leverage it? There is nothing more fruitful than quality one-on-one conversation with someone you admire and respect. However, that is not always possible given schedules and demands. That means you will need to be creative. One idea is to construct your own virtual board of directors, a trusted cadre that meets periodically, in person or virtually, and provides you with support and advice. This virtual board—formal or informal—is your regular place to check-in for feedback, ideas, news and encouragement. Thinking about launching a business? Pondering going back to school for that law degree? These are the people whose opinions you would actively solicit. Additional creative ideas include:

- *Personal mentoring or coaching.* Ask one or two of your key contacts if they would consent to having regular conversations to discuss your choices and your progress. Some will feel more useful to you if they can share what they know in a more intimate setting.

- *Do a remote interview.* This is one of my favorite techniques, particularly for people who are extremely difficult to schedule. Send them targeted questions and ask them to speak their answers and record themselves on their computers or smart phones. Questions might include, "What personal principle has contributed the most to your career success, and how?" While you might have to send a few reminders, eventually they will reply. The revealing, candid answers you'll get will be invaluable. To make this technique even more effective, politely ask if you can periodically update your contact about how their advice is making a positive difference in your life. Supporters love to hear when, and how, their advice is working.

- *Contribute to what they care about.* Get involved in the causes or charities that motivate the people you're reaching out to. This is a terrific way to garner their attention and create goodwill at the same time. Odds are there is at least one that speaks to your personal passion as well.

Bottom line, look for good people with whom you can connect, be open, sincere and genuine, and allow the relationship to develop organically. If the organic development feels a little slow, give it a little nudge. But rest assured, if you are identifying the right people, the relationship will mature over time.

Are You Aiming High Enough?
All of this begs the question: how do you know if you're aiming high enough to reach your dream? First of all, does the magnitude of your dream make you feel a little uncomfortable? As I detailed in Chapter One, feelings of discomfort are often signs that you are pushing the boundaries enough to bring about real change. So if your dreams have you restless yet excited, worried but also eager to test yourself, then you are probably operating in the right zone.

Beyond that, examine how conventional your present journey is. Are you following the same road as everyone else, or are you charting your own course and paying little mind to others' opinions? For example, some may suggest the traditional method to secure a plum job as a software developer in Silicon Valley is to earn an advanced degree in computer science from MIT. But what if you did not do that? What if you were a self-taught programmer with a few community college courses under your belt but world-class skills, who decided to aim for the same high-level software developer job as the MIT grad? You would probably run into a wall of doubt and resistance, but does that mean you should not apply? Absolutely not. You should apply without reservation! Doubts are a sign that you are pushing things enough to be a provocateur. Remember, this is your dream, and nobody has the power to take your dream from you…unless you give it to them.

Are you constantly stimulated by the prospect of what you are trying to achieve? If it is constantly stretching you and forcing you to get the maximum from yourself, your answer should be "Yes". That is one of the reasons so many entrepreneurs continue starting new companies after they successfully exit their original company: they relish the challenge. Work that is mundane and safe will not fire those novelty neurons; dreams that are risky and push the edges of your capacity will. That might mean writing an experimental screenplay that makes Hollywood studio executives reimagine the possibilities of film, or designing a new bicycle prototype that looks like it's from the 22nd century.

Finally, what happens when your dreams or ideas come to fruition? Will that success mean learning to thrive in a world you are totally unfamiliar with? Will it mean stretching yourself beyond your current limits? Do you find yourself saying, "Certainly, I can do that," going into a low-grade panic saying, "Oh no, how do I do that?" and then figuring it out anyway? Aiming high by definition means getting out of your comfort zone and still finding a way to land on your feet. If the prospect of your dreams working out simultaneously terrifies you and makes you feel more alive than ever, you are right where you ought to be.

If you truly believe in who you are and the dreams that you are pursuing, you have all the support you need. When all is said and done, that self-belief is what matters most.

Summary

- *Bold dreams will encounter opposition from insecure people.*

- *If you are not experiencing some opposition, you may not be aiming high enough.*

- *People have expectations that they expect you to fulfill. They expect you to be as you have always been. When you transcend those expectations, do not expect everyone to understand.*

- *You will have proponents and detractors in your life. The proponents will encourage you and have a genuine interest in your success.*

- *Ignore the detractors; their motivations are usually self-serving.*

- *Fill your life with positive, empowering, supportive people from all walks of life.*

- *Sometimes, we keep detractors in our lives because they are familiar. But you have to carefully guard who keep in your inner circle.*

- *Know the criteria you are looking for within the network of supporters you want to build, and find multiple ways to catalyze that network.*

- *Ultimately, your self-belief is the most important asset you have.*

Questions To Ponder

- *Do you feel that your current dreams are too high, too low, or just right? Why?*

- *Have you already faced opposition to your dreams? If so, who was it from and why?*

- *Who are the proponents, the supportive people in your life?*

- *Who are the detractors that are always trying to break you down?*

- *Why do you keep those people in your life?*

- *What will you do in the next year to remove detractors— negative, disempowering individuals—from your circle?*

- *What qualities are you seeking in the people who will form your supportive, opportunity-creating inner circle?*

- *How will you morph into a person who attracts their attention?*

- *What will you do to add value to those relationships?*

- *How does the pursuit of your dreams make you feel daily?*

CHAPTER 9

Ready, Set, Go!

*"The true measure of a man is not what he dreams, but what
he aspires to be; a dream is nothing without action. Whether
one fails or succeeds is irrelevant; all that matters is that there
was motion in his life. That alone affects the world."*
— *Mike Norton, White Mountain*

We have almost reached the end of our journey together, and now it is
time to take action and apply what you have learned. That is often easier
said than done. Sometimes we confuse learning—reading a book, listening
to a speaker, watching a documentary—for action. But they are hardly the
same. This book has been all about getting you to tap into the emotional core
of your hunger for your dream and giving you a formula you can use to make
it happen. It begins now.

Do you have a sense of apprehension, intimidation, or doubt as you
face that prospect? That is normal and understandable, and it does not have
to stop you from taking action. Let me share another story that epitomizes
the power of forward motion.

In the summer of 2012, I was honored to serve as the keynote speaker
at the Hugh O' Brien Leadership (HOBY) conference in Bridgeport,
Connecticut. One of the students in the audience was a high school
sophomore, Karlee Picard. At the conclusion of my speech, I issued a
challenge to the students: return to campus and share the leadership lessons
from my speech with their classmates. Unbeknownst to me, Karlee accepted
the challenge with vigor. She returned to Terryville High school, shared

the lessons, single-handedly talked to school administration, staff, and classmates, and orchestrated an all-school assembly. She then personally invited me to speak in front of the entire Terryville student body in March of 2013.

Karlee is a rising leader and an extremely motivated young woman. What sparked her radical "I refused to be denied to realize my dream" action? Read her 2013 college application essay for some incredible insight:

Once stated by the legendary boxer, Muhammad Ali, "In this world, success comes to those with confidence and faith in themselves." Two years ago, I was a shy high school sophomore that kept to herself and tried her best to stay under the radar. However, after attending the Hugh O'Brian Youth Leadership Conference, I gained a new self-confidence and began truly to realize my potential and impact towards my family, school, and community.

Imagine walking through a wide set of double doors, into a large room full of students foreign to me, and hearing loud, upbeat cheers about HOBY, each one coming from a different direction. My fear was profound, but it quickly diminished over those three transformative days. From the instant I walked through those doors, my life began to change. At first, I only mingled with the individuals closest to me, despite feeling utterly uncomfortable. However, after being put into small groups, I began to form strong bonds with HOBY ambassadors similar to myself. In addition to creating what I hope to be lifelong relationships, I learned useful life skills, such as money management and collaborative learning, all while experiencing college life on the University of Bridgeport campus.

While sharing our philosophies, ideas, and opinions with one another, my group succeeded during the "Free Market

Challenge." Throughout this challenge, we worked in a diverse group, while learning how to use limited resources and money to achieve a common goal. Working in a group of ten people, our objective was to build a marketable product with minimal resources while staying within our budget. While having fun, I learned to work collaboratively with my peers from other schools to create a successful invention.

By far, the most monumental experience during my time at HOBY occurred while listening to our keynote speaker and executive at Ares Management, Ramsey Jay, Jr. Mr. Jay spoke about his life and his story of how he rose to success. Mr. Jay's speech brought tears to the eyes of the audience and was living proof that no matter how your life begins, everyone has an equal opportunity and can make a difference in the world. Without a doubt, Mr. Jay taught me critical lessons that I will take with me through life. The one piece of advice that I clung to was that it was always impossible to do something until someone made it possible.

I was able to apply Mr. Jay's teachings during my junior year in high school. Through six months of effort, I organized for Mr. Jay to come from Los Angeles, California to Terryville, Connecticut to speak to my entire school. I even had the privilege to introduce him to my school before his presentation. I never believed that I would be able to contact an individual awarded with the title of EBONY Magazine's top "30 young leaders under 30", but after Mr. Jay's inspiring speech at HOBY, I had the courage to pursue my dream, and against all odds, I accomplished this endeavor. Every time I feel as if something is impossible, I need to hold my head high and realize that anything is possible.

I am honored and privileged to have been selected by Terryville High School as their HOBY ambassador of 2012.

My experience at HOBY taught me imperative lessons. I gained self-confidence and self-respect. Realizing that I have the power to achieve anything opened my eyes to see my purpose in this world as an individual that has the capability to achieve the impossible.

Light Your Fire

I find that essay flattering and moving beyond words. What did Karlee do to set off the cascade of positive events? She was fearful and filled with anxiety, but she set it aside, stepped out of her comfort zone and put herself in a position to give her dream a chance. What she experienced during those few days at HOBY changed her view of the world, her view of herself, and her belief in what she could accomplish. She had an epiphany. The young woman who departed from the University of Bridgeport campus was not the same one who arrived there.

What Karlee discovered is a truth that is accessible to you: you are equipped to create the life you want, right now. You are all you need. You need not adopt a new identity or become smarter or braver. You have everything you need in you at this moment to take the kind of decisive action to make your dream a reality.

Of course, over time you will need assets that you do not currently possess. You might need an advanced degree, professional certification, training from a skilled mentor, or hands-on experience. But none of those things are necessary to start the process of chasing your dream: to challenge the status quo, take an innovative product to the market, transform yourself into an "A" student, or create a foundation to provide scholarships for deserving students. All you need to begin is to leverage what is in you, and to do that you need to be the spark that lights your own fire…like Karlee.

There is no magic to this. You simply need to have confidence in yourself and put yourself in situations where you will meet new people, encounter outrageous ideas, and discover how others before you have changed their lives. Go to leadership conferences. Run those crazy mud and fire endurance races. Attend publishing or filmmaking workshops. Go on a writer's retreat or join the Peace Corps for a year. Volunteer with local groups to make a difference in the lives of your neighbors—cleaning up streets, repairing houses, whatever it takes. Write a letter to your congressional representative in consideration of a cause you care about. Run for office even if being elected seems like a long shot (recall that President Abraham Lincoln suffered eight political defeats *before* being elected the 16th President of the United States).

You see the pattern? The more you get out there, the more you will learn and the more likely you will meet someone who will set your spirit ablaze. You will find inspiration, help and wisdom in the most unlikely places. Resist the urge to just do what comes easily; seek avenues that require you to improve your weaknesses. Speaking is my God-given gift, and because I know it is a gift, I work extremely hard to refine it. But it does not come easily to everyone. Many people are terrified of public speaking. If you are, become a member of the school debate club or join Toastmasters. Run headlong into your fear and trample it. You will meet amazing people and find energy that you never knew you had.

Shots of Wisdom

God has blessed me with an extraordinary gift: the ability to see inspiration and lessons everywhere I look. That is the byproduct of looking past the circumstances and into the heart of why people do things. If you can train yourself to do the same, you will unearth role models and enlightenment in the seemingly ordinary: a mother's kiss for her child, an act of kindness by a stranger. Try it. It will change how you see the world.

Just Ask

How far can a little daring and a belief that anything is possible take you? Try this as an example. Today, Trooper Sanders is the founder of WiseWhisper, a consultancy that helps organizations develop their philanthropic endeavors. He was also White House and philanthropic advisor to Michelle Obama, former President Bill Clinton, and former Vice President Al Gore. But before all that, Trooper and I worked together at Operation HOPE. One night over dinner, I asked him how one becomes a key advisor to the President of the United States. His answer both surprised and delighted me.

The pivotal moment in Trooper's journey goes back to his first internship in London, in the office of the Prince of Wales, working on major corporate citizenship initiatives. Through that experience, Trooper learned about a similar position with Vice President Gore. After excelling in his role with Vice President Gore, he was able to source the opportunity to work with Mr. Clinton. But the most profound thing was that the office of the Prince of Wales never posted an opening for an intern. That detail did not stop Trooper. He expressed his interest in working for the Prince, figuring the worst thing that could happen is that the staff would say "No." However, they said, "Yes."

If you do not ask, the answer will always be no. Trooper's willingness to ask set off a chain of breakthrough opportunities that, when combined with his brilliance and relationship-building prowess, has allowed him to enjoy extraordinary success. Do you think you could make the same leap of faith, even if there was no posted opening for what you wanted?

The point of the story is that finding people who will help you often just means asking. However, we are frequently our own greatest obstacles. We make the mistake of assuming that everybody has an angle; everybody wants something and assume that a few people are altruistic and good-hearted. But the opposite is true. I know many accomplished, successful people—artists and writers, lawyers and CEOs, scientists and professors—who are generous with their time and genuinely love to help those who approach them for advice or mentorship. The world around you is full of people who will help you—sometimes, to an amazing extent.

But you have to ask for support. If you do, and you hear "No", then your courage and chutzpah will earn respect. You just might find someone who says, "We do not have anything here, but I know someone who might." When you open a door, it is difficult to close it. Hearing the word "no" is not fatal, but failing to ask can be. So why not ask? You have nothing to lose and so much to gain.

Quote

"Never underestimate the power of dreams and the influence of the human spirit. We are all the same in this notion: The potential for greatness lives within each of us."

—*Wilma Rudolph*

The Essentials

This is the sum total of the wisdom I have to offer. With God's blessing in the coming years I will learn and be able to share much more. But before we part ways, let's recap the essential points of this book, in the hope that they may become the building blocks of your dreams.

First, get *comfortable being uncomfortable*. Great things happen when you overcome your fear and try the things that make you nervous or anxious. You are capable of so much more than you realize. An uncomfortable experience might even reveal a new dream that resonates in your spirit—one that would have remained dormant otherwise.

Connect with your *powerful motivating emotions*. The best way to break the natural sense of inertia and get yourself moving is to tap into those feelings that leave you no choice but to take action.

One of the best ways I believe you do that is the Quintessential Motivator. Think about that one person who has always been there for you, always believed in you and never given up on you. Think about meeting that person in 20 years and updating them on what you have done with their selfless sacrifices on your behalf. Making that person proud can be a mighty motivational force.

Identify your *role models*. They have done what you want to do, faced the choices you will be facing, and come through with life-changing testimonies. Remember, you do not need to know your role models. They can be people you admire whose steps you know well enough to follow: elected officials, professional athletes, entrepreneurs, artists, corporate executives, musicians, and the like.

However, role models can also be people whose wisdom and character exceed their material accomplishments. An uncle who donates his time to the less fortunate, a pastor who grew up in poverty and self-funded his seminary study, a teacher who is wise and kind and patient—these are all wonderful role models to emulate. Your role models make it easier to begin changing things in the real world; study what they have done and implement the best of those lessons yourself.

Next, the 3Ps methodology. The first: *Possible*. Before you can change a single thing about your life and pursue your dream, you have to believe that change is possible. Many people become apathetic about their lives, assuming that nothing will ever change, even deciding that they deserve their present fate. But life is what you make of it, and if you decide that nothing will ever change, you will be right. Tap into your powerful emotions and use those as fuel for believing that things can change.

The second P is *Probable*. Once you accept that your dreams can happen, you have to put in extraordinary work to increase the odds that they *will* happen. You go to college or technical school. You get an internship. You train with a mentor. You read everything on your desired field. You practice for endless hours. You network and meet people who can help you. You polish and refine your personal presentation. And you develop a routine, a disciplined practice that earns you mastery of your skill set.

Finally, *Predictable*. Prepare a routine—a lifestyle—that produces excellence again and again *before* a breakthrough opportunity presents itself. The point is to transform into someone for whom success is natural, even inevitable. Predictability means preparing so vigorously that you can replicate the best aspects of yourself in any situation and always perform your best when opportunity knocks and the pressure is on. In every networking scenario, you are poised, erudite, charming and generous. In every interview, you are sharp, prepared, brilliant and surprising. In every position you take, you are resourceful, assertive, a creative thinker and a natural leader.

What Else?

Consider joining local business incubators or success round tables, which cater to ambitious people from all walks of life. In most cities you can find gatherings for entrepreneurs, financial professionals, creative artists, and more. They typically combine brainstorming and support with things like job fairs, training and even access to investors. Don't think you have anything to contribute? How about your experience, intellect and unique perspective?

Final Pieces of the Puzzle

Once you have prepared your predictable practices, look at the *people in your life*. Remember that hearing "No" and facing opposition as you pursue your dreams is a good sign, but at the same time you do not want detractors becoming embedded in your life. Instead, seek proponents who fill you up, take pride in what you do and believe in you. Take steps to become someone who attracts positive people. Be generous, be a problem solver, be optimistic and confident.

One of the characteristics most respected by those who have achieved success is resilience, the ability to bounce back after failure. They respect resilience because every one of them has failed, usually more than once, often spectacularly. A setback is a setup for a comeback if you get up!

Remember that attracting proponents is a matter of being a person they want to know. It is also about building a diverse network. You are not just after captains of industry or technology innovators, but fashion designers, ministers, poets and carpenters. Fill your world with people of character and values and they will fill you up in return.

Then it is time to *take extraordinary action*. Extraordinary people are merely ordinary men and women who found the fortitude and vision to do extraordinary things. We are what we do. Advance your dreams by taking bold, aggressive steps. Do not fear failure; failure is one of life's greatest teachers.

Your actions will help you *tell your story* in a new way. The story you tell not only shapes how other people view you, but also how you view yourself. Both halves of your story—how you arrived where you are today and where you are going from today on—are important. If you can see the value and lessons in your past, you can find the purpose in your future.

Finally, *never quit*. Never stop believing in your power to change and impact the world. Every person who has become a leader began where you are now—with doubt, fear and confusion over what to do next. Significant achievements are often only recognized in hindsight; we do what we do to serve others, honor our values and live our dreams to the best of our ability. If we are true to ourselves, we might be called "great". But now, all you need to do is believe in your dreams, follow your passion, and never compromise your character or values.

Now, get up and take that first step. Shake things up. Follow your dream. Write your new story. I have faith it will have a marvelous ending.

Summary

- *It is hard to start making changes. But if you can overcome your fear and take the first step, you will find that you can keep moving forward.*

- *Getting uncomfortable improves your odds of encountering something that ignites your fire and motivates you.*

- *Get out there—trade shows, conferences, festivals, you name it. Meet people, learn and engage. New doors of opportunity open all the time.*

- *Always ask. The worst that can happen is "No". But you just might hear a 'yes'. You are guaranteed "No" if you do not ask.*

- *People respect courage and audacity, and they are more altruistic than you think. They will assist you.*

Questions To Ponder

- *What now? What is your first step?*

- *What opportunities do you have to get a little uncomfortable, put yourself out there, and be forced to adapt?*

- *What ignites your fire?*

- *Are you willing to ask for outrageous opportunities? Why or why not?*

- *What lesson from this book has been most useful to you and how are you applying it?*

- *What are you going to do to stay on course and reach your dreams?*